This Textbook is useful for Savitribai Phule Pune University and other Universities of Maharashtra as well as Competitive Exams.

Advanced Marketing
(Branding)
(Course Code : BR575MJ)

M.Com.- I (Sem. - II)

As per New Education Policy (2020)

Dr. Mangesh P. Waghmare
(BE., MBA., NET., SET., PGDIBO., LLB., Ph.D.)
New Arts, Commerce & Science College, Ahmednagar.

Dr. Vijay D. Nirmal
(M.Com., M. Phil., SET., Ph.D.)
Padmashri Vikhe Patil College of ACS., Pravaranagar.

Dr. Vidya Mithare
(M.Com., SET., Ph.D.)
Haribhai V. Desai College of Commerce, Arts and Science, Pune.

Dr. Shriprakash Soni
(MBA., Ph.D.)
Haribhai V. Desai College of Commerce, Arts and Science, Pune.

2024

AF517998

Price: 80/-

SUCCESS PUBLICATIONS

Published by
Dr. Rajesh M. Patne
Success Publications
Radha Krishna Apartment, 535, Shaniwar Peth,
Appa Balwant Chowk, Opp. Prabhat Talkies, Pune - 411 030.
Mobile: 9325315464, 8390848833

Edition
2024

Edited By
Mr. Valmik Gaikwad

Typesetting, Layout
Miss. Sayali Bhosale

Cover Designing
Miss. Varsha Lokhande

ISBN NO. – 978-81-19939-26-8

Preface

It is a matter of great pleasure for us to present this book to our esteemed readers. This book has been designed as standard text on 'Advanced Marketing (Branding) (Course Code BR575MJ)' for M.Com. (Sem. - II).

This book comprehensively covers the entire syllabus of M.Com. (Advanced Marketing (Branding) Course of Savitribai Phule Pune University effective from 2023 onwards. It has been written to meet the requirements of students of M.Com. Some of the special features of the book are as follows:

1. *Full coverage of the revised syllabus of M.Com.*
2. *Chapter outline at the beginning of each chapter to give a bird's eye view of the topics covered in the chapter.*
3. *Point wise explanation of each topic in the chapter.*
4. *Topics are logically arranged in numbered paragraphs exactly according to the modified syllabus.*
5. *Proposed questions at the end of each chapter.*
6. *Extensive use of diagrams, tables and various forms to give visual view of key concepts and techniques.*
7. *Conversational, lucid and simple language.*

Every effort has been made to provide the readers with most up-to-date and authentic material on the subject.

We are very grateful to our publisher Mrs. and Mr. Rajesh Patne who have rendered all possible assistance in bringing out this book. We wish to acknowledge our deep gratitude to staff who have assisted and helped us in preparing this book. We will consider our efforts amply rewarded in case the book proves useful to the students and teachers of the subject.

Suggestions of readers are welcome and shall be acknowledged with gratitude.

With best wishes.

By Authors

Syllabus

M.Com. - I (Sem. - II) Advanced Marketing

Branding (Course Code : BR575MJ)

Unit No.	Topic	No. of Periods
1	**Introduction to Branding** Branding: Meaning and Definition, Features and Importance. Brand Planning, Brand elements, Steps of brand building process, Impact of brands in markets, society and business, Branding challenge and opportunities, Essential brand components, The importance of consumer perception and behavior in branding.	15
2	**Brand building** Meaning and Importance, Brand building Strategies, The impact of advertising in building brand equity, marketing communications and the brand building, Growing and sustaining brands, Process internal branding, New brand launches, rebranding. Types of branding, Branding in graphic design, Branding in the age of social media.	15

INDEX

M.Com. - I (Sem. - II) Advanced Marketing

Branding (Course Code : BR575MJ)

UNIT 1

Introduction to Branding

Introduction:

Branding encapsulates the art and science of crafting a distinctive identity that not only sets a product, service, or company apart but also forges a lasting connection with its audience. It's the holistic orchestration of tangible and intangible elements ranging from logos, colors, and typography to values, narratives, and emotional resonance that collectively form the essence of a brand. Beyond mere visuals, branding embodies the promise delivered consistently, evoking emotions, building trust, and fostering loyalty. It's the sum of experiences, perceptions, and associations that stakeholders attach to a brand, influencing their decision-making process. Effective branding extends beyond recognition, breathing life into a unique story that resonates with the target market, establishing an enduring relationship that transcends transactions, ultimately driving loyalty and advocacy.

1.1 Branding:

Branding is the intricate process of crafting a distinct and memorable identity for a product, service, or company. It's the sum of every impression, emotion, and association that people connect with a particular entity. Beyond logos and visuals, branding encompasses the personality, values, and promises that differentiate one from others, leaving a lasting imprint on consumers' minds. Successful branding not only cultivates recognition but also builds trust, loyalty, and an emotional bond with the audience. It's the art of storytelling, creating an experience that resonates deeply, influencing consumer choices and fostering enduring relationships, ultimately driving sustained success and growth.

1.1.1 Meaning:

Branding refers to the process of creating a distinctive and recognizable identity for a product, service, or organization. It involves shaping perceptions, emotions, and associations around that entity through various means such as logos, messaging, values, and experiences. Effective branding goes beyond just visual elements; it aims to establish a connection with the audience, building trust, loyalty, and a strong emotional bond. It's about crafting a story, evoking feelings, and influencing how people perceive and interact with a brand, ultimately impacting their choices and fostering lasting relationships.

1.1.2 Definitions:

Following are the definitions of Branding:

1) **Philip Kotler:**

   "A brand is a name, term, sign, symbol, or design, or a combination of them, intended to identify the goods or services of one seller or group of sellers and to differentiate them from those of competitors."

2) **David Aaker:**

   "A brand is a set of assets and liabilities linked to a name and symbol that adds to (or subtracts from) the value provided by a product or service."

3) **Seth Godin:**

   "A brand is the set of expectations, memories, stories, and relationships that, taken together, account for a consumer's decision to choose one product or service over another."

4) **Al Ries and Jack Trout:**

   "A brand is not just a logo or a product, it is the perception that lives in the mind of the customer."

1.1.3 Features of Branding:

Following facets forms a critical component of effective branding, intertwining to shape a brand's identity, perception, and relationship with its audience in a dynamic and competitive market landscape.

1) **Identity and Differentiation:**

At the heart of branding lies the creation of a unique identity. Brands strive to stand out in a crowded marketplace by developing distinct features that set them apart. This differentiation can manifest through various elements such as logos, color schemes, taglines, and brand messaging. A brand's identity acts as its visual and conceptual fingerprint, serving as a beacon that helps consumers recognize and distinguish it from competitors. For instance, Apple's sleek and minimalist design language and iconic bitten apple logo instantly differentiate its products in the tech landscape, fostering a strong brand identity.

2) **Consistency and Cohesion:**

Branding relies on consistency across all touchpoints to build and maintain trust with consumers. Every interaction is it through advertising, customer service, product quality, or social media should reflect the brand's values, tone, and personality. This cohesion strengthens the brand's identity, reinforces its messaging, and cultivates a sense of reliability and familiarity among consumers. Consider how Coca-Cola maintains consistency in its branding, from its classic red color scheme to its timeless "Open Happiness" campaign, establishing a cohesive brand image globally.

3) **Emotional Connection:**

Successful branding transcends mere transactions by forging emotional connections with consumers. Brands aim to evoke specific emotions or associations linked to their products or services. By tapping into consumers' feelings, aspirations, or values, brands create a deeper bond that goes beyond the functional aspects of their offerings. Nike, with its "Just Do It" slogan and powerful storytelling in ad campaigns, taps into the emotional aspects of motivation and determination, resonating with consumers on a personal level.

4) **Brand Promise and Trust:**

Central to effective branding is the establishment of a brand promise—a commitment or assurance to consumers about what they can expect. This promise encompasses the brand's values, quality, and overall experience it aims to deliver. Consistently fulfilling this promise builds trust and credibility, crucial for sustaining long-term relationships with consumers. For instance, Volvo's brand promise of safety has been a cornerstone of its identity, fostering trust among consumers who prioritize safety in automobile choices.

5) **Brand Equity and Value:**

Branding contributes significantly to a brand's equity and perceived value. Brand equity encapsulates the intangible value a brand holds, encompassing consumer perception, loyalty, and the premium a consumer might be willing to pay for that brand over others. A strong brand like Disney, built over decades through storytelling, quality entertainment, and a magical experience, commands high brand equity, allowing it to extend its reach into various industries and command premium pricing.

6) **Target Audience Understanding:**

Effective branding hinges on a deep understanding of the target audience. Brands conduct extensive research to grasp their consumers' demographics, preferences, behaviors, and desires. This knowledge enables brands to tailor their messaging, products, and experiences to resonate with their audience, fostering a more meaningful connection. Consider how luxury brands like Chanel or Rolex understand their affluent audience's desires for exclusivity and craftsmanship, shaping their branding accordingly.

7) **Innovation and Adaptability:**

Brands need to evolve and adapt to changing market dynamics while staying true to their core identity. Innovation plays a pivotal role in keeping brands relevant and fresh in consumers' minds. Successful brands embrace innovation, whether in product development, marketing strategies, or technological advancements, to meet evolving consumer needs and preferences. Apple's consistent innovation in technology and design has kept the brand at the forefront of the industry, continually captivating consumers with new products and experiences.

8) **Storytelling and Narrative:**

Compelling storytelling lies at the heart of effective branding. Brands craft narratives that engage and resonate with their audience, weaving stories that communicate their values, mission, and purpose. Through storytelling, brands create an emotional connection, humanize their identity, and leave a lasting impact on consumers. For example, Airbnb's storytelling focuses on the idea of belonging, fostering connections, and the unique experiences their platform enables, aligning with their brand's ethos.

9) **Brand Culture and Internal Alignment:**

Brands that succeed in external branding often have a strong internal brand culture. Employees play a vital role in delivering the brand promise and experience. A cohesive brand culture aligns employees' values and behaviors with the brand's values, ensuring a consistent delivery of the brand's promise at every touchpoint. Companies like Google foster an internal culture that aligns with their innovative, boundary-pushing external brand image, attracting top talent and reinforcing their brand's identity.

10) **Adaptability to Digital Landscape:**

In today's digital age, branding extends beyond traditional channels to encompass online platforms and social media. Brands need to adapt their strategies to the digital landscape, engaging with consumers in real-time, fostering communities, and leveraging the power of social media influencers. Brands like Wendy's have mastered the art of social media engagement, utilizing witty and engaging content to connect with their audience, enhancing brand visibility and relevance in the digital sphere.

1.1.4 Importance of Branding:

Following aspects collectively highlight the multifaceted significance of branding, illustrating its pivotal role in shaping consumer perceptions, driving business success, and fostering enduring relationships with customers and stakeholders.

1) **Differentiation and Recognition:**

   Branding serves as a powerful tool for differentiation in a competitive market landscape. It helps distinguish a product, service, or company from its competitors by creating a unique identity. A well-established brand with a distinct logo, color scheme, and messaging stands out, enabling consumers to recognize and remember it amidst a sea of options. For instance, the iconic Nike swoosh or McDonald's golden arches are instantly recognizable symbols, showcasing the power of effective branding in creating lasting impressions.

2) **Consumer Trust and Loyalty:**

   Building trust and fostering customer loyalty are crucial aspects of branding. A strong brand that consistently delivers on its promises and maintains quality standards cultivates trust among consumers. Trust forms the bedrock of long-term relationships with customers, encouraging repeat purchases and positive word-of-mouth referrals. Brands like Amazon, known for reliability and customer-centric services, have earned immense loyalty due to their consistent brand experience.

3) **Market Positioning and Competitive Edge:**

   Branding plays a pivotal role in defining a brand's position in the market. A well-crafted brand strategy helps carve out a distinct space in consumers' minds, positioning the brand in a way that highlights its unique value proposition. This positioning contributes to gaining a competitive edge by emphasizing what sets the brand apart. For example, Volvo's emphasis on safety has positioned it as a leader in automobile safety, giving it a competitive advantage over other car manufacturers.

4) **Increased Financial Value:**

   Brands with strong recognition and positive associations often possess higher financial value. Brand equity, which encompasses the perceived value of a brand, influences consumer behavior and their willingness to pay a premium for the brand's products or services. Companies with valuable brands like Apple or Coca-Cola command higher prices and market share, showcasing the direct link between branding and financial success.

5) **Emotional Connection and Engagement:**

Effective branding goes beyond functional aspects and connects with consumers on an emotional level. Brands that evoke emotions or align with consumers' values create deeper connections, leading to stronger brand loyalty. Emotional branding strategies, like those employed by brands such as Dove or Subaru, resonate with consumers' emotions, fostering stronger bonds and engagement.

6) **Facilitating Expansion and Diversification:**

Strong brands have the potential to extend their presence into new markets or product categories. A well-established brand's credibility and recognition can ease the entry into new ventures or the introduction of new products. For instance, Google expanded from its search engine roots into various technological domains due to the trust and brand equity it built over time.

7) **Consistency and Reliability:**

Consistency in branding is crucial for establishing reliability and predictability. Brands that maintain a consistent image, message, and quality across all touchpoints instill confidence in consumers. This consistency reinforces the brand's values and promises, fostering trust and reliability. Brands like FedEx, known for their consistent service quality and reliable delivery, have successfully built their reputation based on consistency.

8) **Employee Alignment and Brand Advocacy:**

A strong brand not only resonates with consumers but also inspires employees. Brands with a clear mission and values create a sense of purpose among employees, fostering a strong internal brand culture. Engaged employees who believe in the brand become advocates, delivering consistent brand experiences and positively influencing the brand's perception.

9) **Brand Resilience in Times of Crisis:**

A well-established brand with a positive reputation can weather crises more effectively. Brands that have built strong relationships with their consumers through consistent and trustworthy behavior are more likely to receive support and understanding during challenging times. For instance, brands like Toyota and Tylenol rebounded successfully from past crises due to their strong brand equity and transparent communication.

10) **Long-Term Business Growth and Sustainability:**

Branding contributes significantly to a company's long-term growth and sustainability. A strong brand serves as a foundation for continued success, driving customer acquisition, retention, and overall business growth. Brands that invest in nurturing their brand equity and delivering consistent experiences position themselves for sustained success in the ever-evolving market landscape.

1.2 Brand Planning:

Brand planning involves a comprehensive process of strategizing, outlining, and implementing a roadmap that defines a brand's objectives, target audience, positioning, and tactics to achieve its goals. It encompasses meticulous research to understand market dynamics, consumer behavior, and competitive landscapes, enabling the formulation of a clear brand strategy. This planning phase involves setting specific, measurable, achievable, relevant, and time-bound (SMART) goals, identifying unique selling propositions, crafting brand messaging, designing brand experiences, and establishing guidelines for consistent implementation across various touchpoints. Brand planning serves as the foundational framework that guides all brand-related decisions, ensuring alignment with the brand's vision, values, and long-term objectives while adapting to evolving market trends and consumer needs.

1.2.1 Meaning:

Brand planning refers to the systematic process of devising a strategic framework that defines a brand's essence, direction, and objectives. It involves in-depth analysis of market insights, consumer behavior, and competitive landscapes to craft a roadmap that outlines the brand's positioning, messaging, and tactics for achieving its goals. This planning phase encompasses setting clear objectives, identifying target audiences, delineating unique brand propositions, and establishing guidelines for consistent implementation across various channels. Brand planning acts as a compass, guiding all brand-related decisions and actions, ensuring cohesion, resonance, and relevance in the dynamic marketplace.

1.2.2 Definitions:

Following are the definitions of Brand Planning:

1) **Kapferer and Bastien:**

   "Brand planning is the strategic thinking process that shapes and guides the entire organization. It aligns business objectives with consumer needs, aspirations, and market realities to create a sustainable competitive advantage."

2) **Kevin Lane Keller:**

   "Brand planning is the deliberate process of defining the brand's purpose, values, and position in the market. It involves setting clear objectives, identifying target segments, and crafting strategies to achieve brand resonance."

3) **David Aaker:**

   "Brand planning is the systematic approach to developing and implementing brand strategies that leverage the brand's assets and create brand equity. It involves defining the brand's identity, establishing differentiation, and managing brand portfolios to drive long-term success."

1.2.3 Process of Brand Planning:

Process of brand planning explained with following points:

1) **Understanding Business Objectives:**
This initial step in brand planning involves a comprehensive review of the company's overarching goals, mission, and vision. It requires aligning brand strategies with the broader business objectives. By deeply understanding these objectives, brand planners can develop strategies that not only resonate with the target audience but also contribute to the company's growth and sustainability. This stage involves engaging stakeholders across departments to ensure a holistic understanding of the organization's aspirations and direction.

2) **Market Research and Analysis:**
Market research forms the bedrock of effective brand planning. It involves a meticulous analysis of market trends, consumer behavior, competitor strategies, and potential opportunities or threats in the industry. This in-depth understanding assists in identifying market gaps, emerging trends, and consumer needs, offering insights crucial for developing a competitive brand strategy that resonates with the target audience.

3) **Defining Brand Identity and Values:**
Defining the brand's identity involves establishing its personality, core values, and unique propositions. It's about determining what the brand stands for, its ethos, and the emotional connection it aims to establish with consumers. By clearly defining these elements, brand planners can shape a cohesive brand image that communicates the brand's essence consistently across all touchpoints.

4) **Target Audience Segmentation:**
Segmenting the target audience involves dividing consumers into distinct groups based on demographics, behaviors, preferences, and needs. This segmentation facilitates tailored communication strategies that resonate with each group's unique characteristics and desires. Understanding these segments enables brands to personalize messaging, products, and experiences, ensuring a more effective connection with the audience.

5) **Brand Positioning Strategy:**
Establishing the brand's positioning involves determining its place in the market landscape and how it differentiates itself from competitors. This strategy outlines the unique value proposition that the brand offers to its audience. It defines the space the brand aims to occupy in the minds of consumers, highlighting its strengths and key attributes while addressing consumer needs or pain points.

6) **Creating Brand Messaging and Communication Strategies:**
Crafting compelling brand messages and communication strategies involves translating the brand's identity, values, and positioning into resonant messages. It

encompasses developing a brand narrative, taglines, and communication plans that effectively convey the brand's story and value proposition to the target audience across various channels and platforms.

7) **Visual Identity Development:**

Visual identity development involves designing the brand's visual elements, such as the logo, color palette, typography, and overall aesthetics. These visual components play a significant role in brand recognition and recall. Consistency in visual elements across all brand assets and communication materials helps reinforce the brand's identity and strengthen its visual appeal.

8) **Implementation and Activation Plans:**

Once the brand strategies are defined, an implementation plan outlines how these strategies will be executed across various channels and touchpoints. This involves detailing marketing campaigns, advertising initiatives, digital presence, PR activities, and other promotional plans aimed at introducing the brand effectively to the market and its target audience.

9) **Monitoring and Evaluation:**

Continuous monitoring and evaluation are critical to assess the effectiveness of brand initiatives. Key performance indicators (KPIs) are established to measure the success of branding efforts. Regularly tracking these metrics, gathering feedback, and conducting market analyses enable brands to make informed decisions, identify areas for improvement, and refine strategies to maintain relevance and resonance with the audience.

10) **Brand Evolution and Adaptation:**

Brand planning is an ongoing process that requires adaptability and evolution over time. Brands need to remain agile and responsive to changes in consumer preferences, market dynamics, and industry trends. Regular assessments, reassessments, and revisions ensure that the brand stays aligned with evolving market needs while staying true to its core identity and values. This adaptability ensures the brand remains relevant and maintains a competitive edge in the market landscape.

1.2.4 Factors Influencing Brand Planning:

Following factors represents a critical aspect that brands must consider when developing comprehensive brand planning strategies, ensuring relevance, adaptability, and resonance in an ever-evolving marketplace.

1) **Market Analysis and Insights:**

A crucial factor shaping brand planning is a comprehensive understanding of the market landscape. This involves analyzing market trends, consumer behavior, competitors' strategies, and emerging opportunities. By diving into these insights, brands can identify market gaps, consumer preferences, and unmet needs, laying the foundation for informed strategic decisions. For instance, thorough market analysis might reveal a shift in consumer preferences towards eco-friendly products, prompting a brand to incorporate sustainability into its planning to meet this growing demand.

2) **Consumer Behavior and Preferences:**

Central to brand planning is an in-depth understanding of consumer behavior and preferences. Brands need to comprehend what motivates their target audience, their purchase patterns, values, and desires. This insight helps tailor products, messaging, and experiences to align with consumer expectations, creating resonance and fostering stronger connections. For instance, a tech brand understanding the increasing consumer preference for user-friendly interfaces might prioritize ease of use in their product development and marketing strategies.

3) **Competitive Landscape:**

Analysis of competitors' strategies, strengths, weaknesses, and market positioning is crucial in brand planning. Understanding how competitors operate, their marketing tactics, and their unique selling propositions helps brands differentiate themselves effectively. It allows brands to identify gaps or opportunities to position themselves uniquely and communicate their distinct value propositions to stand out in the market.

4) **Technological Advancements:**

Rapid technological advancements continually shape consumer behavior and market dynamics. Brands need to incorporate these changes into their planning. Adopting innovative technologies or leveraging digital platforms can enhance customer experiences, streamline operations, and facilitate better engagement. For instance, a brand integrating AI-powered customer service chatbots aligns with the trend toward efficient and personalized customer interactions.

5) **Cultural and Societal Shifts:**

Societal changes and cultural shifts impact consumer perceptions and values. Brands must be attuned to these changes to stay relevant and resonate with their audience. For example, changing attitudes towards inclusivity and diversity might prompt brands to re-evaluate their messaging, ensuring it reflects these evolving societal values in their planning and communication strategies.

6) **Regulatory and Legal Environment:**

Compliance with regulations and legal frameworks significantly influences brand planning. Brands must adhere to industry-specific regulations, consumer privacy laws, advertising standards, and other legal considerations. Adapting to changes in these areas is crucial to avoiding penalties, maintaining trust, and ensuring a positive brand image.

7) **Economic Factors:**

   Economic conditions, such as inflation, market fluctuations, or economic downturns, can impact consumer spending habits and brand strategies. Brands need to factor in these economic dynamics when planning marketing budgets, pricing strategies, and product offerings to remain competitive and adaptable to changing financial landscapes.

8) **Globalization and Market Expansion:**

   For brands eyeing global markets or expanding their reach, globalization plays a pivotal role in brand planning. Understanding diverse cultures, local preferences, and market nuances becomes essential. Adapting branding strategies to resonate with different cultures while maintaining a consistent brand image poses a challenge and opportunity in global brand planning.

9) **Internal Capabilities and Resources:**

   The internal capabilities and resources of a brand significantly influence its planning. Brands need to assess their strengths, weaknesses, available resources, and competencies. This evaluation helps in aligning strategic goals with realistic capabilities, ensuring effective implementation of brand strategies.

10) **Social and Environmental Responsibility:**

    Increasingly, consumers expect brands to take a stance on social and environmental issues. Brands integrating social responsibility and sustainability into their planning not only fulfill ethical obligations but also resonate with socially conscious consumers, positively impacting brand perception and loyalty.

1.2.5 Importance of Brand Planning:

Brand planning serves as the backbone of a brand's strategy, influencing its positioning, consumer perception, growth trajectory, and resilience in a competitive landscape.

1) **Strategic Direction:**

   Brand planning establishes a strategic roadmap that guides the overall direction of a brand. It helps define the brand's vision, mission, values, and long-term objectives. This strategic clarity serves as a compass, ensuring that all brand-related decisions, initiatives, and communications align with a unified purpose. It enables brands to chart a clear path towards achieving their goals and maintaining consistency in their messaging and actions.

2) **Market Differentiation:**

   In a crowded marketplace, effective brand planning is crucial for setting a brand apart from competitors. It involves identifying and leveraging unique selling propositions, key strengths, and distinctive attributes that differentiate the brand. This differentiation fosters brand recognition and recall among consumers, establishing a competitive edge and increasing the brand's relevance in consumers' minds.

3) **Consumer Connection:**
Brand planning focuses on understanding consumer needs, behaviors, and aspirations. By analyzing consumer insights, preferences, and behaviors, brands can develop strategies that resonate with their target audience. This alignment with consumer sentiments fosters a deeper emotional connection, driving brand loyalty, advocacy, and long-term relationships.

4) **Value Proposition:**
Through meticulous brand planning, brands define their value proposition—the unique value they offer to consumers. This encapsulates not only the functional benefits but also the emotional and symbolic attributes that consumers associate with the brand. A compelling value proposition communicates why consumers should choose a particular brand over others, compellingly articulating its benefits and relevance.

5) **Consistency and Trust:**
A well-thought-out brand plan ensures consistency across all brand touchpoints. Consistency in messaging, visual identity, product quality, and customer experience builds trust among consumers. When a brand consistently delivers on its promises and maintains a coherent image, it fosters credibility and reliability, enhancing consumer trust and confidence in the brand.

6) **Long-Term Growth:**
Brand planning contributes significantly to a brand's long-term growth and sustainability. It involves setting achievable yet ambitious goals and devising strategies to achieve them. A strategic approach to brand planning ensures that the brand stays agile, adaptable, and relevant in an ever-evolving market, positioning itself for sustained growth amidst changing consumer preferences and market dynamics.

7) **Brand Resilience:**
Brands equipped with robust brand planning strategies are better equipped to navigate through challenges and crises. By anticipating potential risks and having contingency plans in place, brands can effectively mitigate the impact of adverse situations. A well-established brand with a strong plan is more resilient, maintaining consumer confidence and loyalty during challenging times.

8) **Resource Allocation and Efficiency:**
Brand planning assists in allocating resources - financial, human and technological in an optimal manner. It helps prioritize initiatives and investments that align with the brand's strategic objectives, ensuring efficient utilization of resources. By focusing efforts on areas that contribute most significantly to the brand's success, brand planning maximizes efficiency and effectiveness.

9) **Employee Alignment and Engagement:**

An integral part of brand planning involves aligning internal stakeholders, particularly employees, with the brand's values and objectives. Engaged and motivated employees who understand and believe in the brand's vision become brand ambassadors. They play a pivotal role in delivering consistent brand experiences, fostering positive perceptions, and driving brand advocacy.

10) **Adaptability and Innovation:**

A well-structured brand plan allows brands to remain adaptable and responsive to changing market trends, consumer preferences, and technological advancements. It encourages a culture of innovation, enabling brands to evolve their offerings, experiences, and strategies to stay relevant and competitive in a dynamic marketplace.

1.3 Brand Elements:

Brand elements encompass the identifiable components that collectively form a brand's visual, auditory, and conceptual identity. These elements are the building blocks that consumers associate with a particular brand, facilitating recognition, differentiation, and connection. They include tangible elements like logos, color schemes, typography, symbols, and packaging, which serve as visual cues that trigger immediate brand recall. Additionally, brand elements extend to intangible aspects like brand name, taglines, jingles, and even brand associations, values, and personality. When strategically designed and consistently applied, these elements not only enhance brand visibility but also convey the brand's essence, values, and promises, contributing significantly to a brand's identity and perception in the minds of consumers.

1.3.1 Meaning:

Brand elements refer to the distinctive and identifiable components that compose a brand's visual, auditory, and conceptual identity. These elements encapsulate both tangible and intangible aspects that consumers associate with a specific brand. Tangible elements include visual cues such as logos, color schemes, typography, packaging, and symbols that contribute to immediate brand recognition. On the other hand, intangible elements encompass brand name, taglines, jingles, associations, values, and personality traits. Collectively, these elements work synergistically to create a unique brand identity, fostering consumer loyalty, differentiation from competitors, and a strong emotional connection. By strategically designing and consistently employing these elements across various touchpoints, brands establish a cohesive and memorable identity that resonates with their target audience, shaping consumer perceptions and experiences.

1.3.2 Various Brand Elements:

Brand elements collectively contribute to shaping a brand's identity, creating recognition, differentiation, and emotional resonance in the minds of consumers.

1) **Logo:**

   One of the most recognizable brand elements, a logo is a visual representation of a brand's identity. It's a symbol or graphic mark designed to encapsulate the essence and values of a brand in a visually appealing and memorable way. Logos often incorporate colors, shapes, and typography that evoke specific emotions or associations related to the brand. For instance, the Nike swoosh symbolizes movement and speed, instantly connecting with the brand's athletic identity.

2) **Color Palette:**

   Colors play a significant role in brand identity, as they evoke emotions and convey messages. A brand's chosen color palette influences consumer perception and recognition. For example, the vibrant red of Coca-Cola or the calming blue of Facebook are instantly associated with these brands, reflecting their brand personalities and values.

3) **Typography:**

   The choice of fonts and typography in branding communicates a brand's tone, style, and personality. Whether it's a sleek and modern typeface or a classic and elegant font, typography contributes to the overall visual identity. For instance, the distinct typography of brands like Disney or Coca-Cola contributes significantly to their brand recognition.

4) **Slogan/Tagline:**

   A catchy and memorable slogan or tagline encapsulates a brand's essence or value proposition succinctly. It serves as a verbal cue that reinforces brand messaging and can become synonymous with the brand itself. Think of Nike's "Just Do It" or McDonald's "I'm Lovin' It" these taglines have become inseparable from the brands they represent.

5) **Brand Name:**

   The brand name is a fundamental element, serving as the primary identifier for the brand. It might be a coined word, a descriptive name, or the name of the founder. A well-chosen brand name can resonate with consumers and differentiate the brand in a crowded market. Brands like Apple or Google have made their names synonymous with innovation and technology.

6) **Symbols and Icons:**

   Brands often utilize symbols or icons beyond their logos to represent their identity. These symbols may be cultural or industry-specific, providing an additional visual cue that reinforces brand recognition. For example, the Twitter bird or the Target bullseye are iconic symbols instantly associated with their respective brands.

7) **Packaging Design:**
Packaging serves as a tangible representation of a brand, playing a crucial role in consumer perception and purchase decisions. Effective packaging design not only protects the product but also communicates brand values, personality, and quality. Brands like Apple or Tiffany & Co. are known for their distinctive and luxurious packaging, enhancing the overall brand experience.

8) **Sound Branding:** Auditory elements, such as jingles or specific sounds, contribute to brand recognition and recall.
A well-crafted jingle or sound logo can create a strong emotional connection with consumers and reinforce brand identity. Think of the Intel jingle or the McDonald's "I'm Lovin' It" melody—these auditory cues instantly evoke the associated brands.

9) **Brand Characters or Mascots:**
Some brands use characters or mascots to personify their identity and connect with consumers on a more personal level. These characters often become an integral part of a brand's storytelling and marketing campaigns. For instance, the Michelin Man or the Geico Gecko is iconic brand mascots that enhance brand recall and engagement.

10) **Brand Storytelling and Tone of Voice:**
While not visual elements in the traditional sense, storytelling and tone of voice are essential brand elements. They shape how a brand communicates its messages, values, and narratives. Consistent storytelling and a distinct tone of voice contribute to building a brand's personality and fostering emotional connections with consumers.

1.4 Brand Building Process:

Brand building is a meticulous process that involves the strategic development and nurturing of a brand's identity, perception, and relationships with its audience. It begins with a deep understanding of the market landscape, target audience, and competitive dynamics.

1) **Understanding Target Audience and Market Research:**
The foundation of brand building lies in understanding the target audience. Conducting thorough market research helps identify consumer demographics, preferences, behaviors, and pain points. This insight enables brands to tailor their products, messaging, and strategies to meet specific needs. Understanding the audience's motivations and desires is crucial for creating a brand that resonates with them.

2) **Defining Brand Purpose and Values:**
Establishing the brand's purpose and values forms the core identity. Brands need a clear vision beyond profits, reflecting their beliefs, missions, and commitments. Articulating these values guides decision-making, shapes the brand's personality,

and connects emotionally with consumers. Patagonia, for instance, prioritizes environmental activism, aligning its brand with sustainability and ethical practices.

3) **Crafting Brand Identity:**

Brand identity encompasses visual elements like logos, color schemes, typography, and design styles that represent the brand. It's crucial to create a cohesive and memorable identity that reflects the brand's essence. Consistency across all touchpoints, from packaging to online presence, reinforces brand recall and fosters a strong brand image. Consider Nike's iconic swoosh logo or Apple's minimalist design as examples of powerful brand identities.

4) **Developing Brand Messaging and Positioning:**

Crafting a compelling brand message and positioning strategy is pivotal. It involves communicating the brand's value proposition, unique selling points, and how it differs from competitors. Effective messaging resonates with the target audience, evokes emotions, and solidifies the brand's position in the market. Brands like Airbnb excel in positioning themselves as more than a lodging provider, focusing on unique travel experiences and a sense of belonging.

5) **Building Brand Awareness through Marketing Channels:**

Utilizing various marketing channels and strategies helps in creating brand awareness. From traditional mediums like TV, print, and radio to digital platforms, social media, and influencer collaborations, brands engage with their audience across multiple channels. Consistent messaging and storytelling through these channels contribute to increased visibility and recognition.

6) **Delivering Consistent Brand Experience:**

Ensuring a consistent brand experience across all touchpoints is crucial. From customer interactions to product quality and brand communications, consistency builds trust and credibility. Every interaction should reflect the brand's values, reinforcing the desired perception among consumers. Starbucks, known for its consistent customer experience and coffee quality, exemplifies this approach.

7) **Engaging with the Audience and Creating Relationships:**

Building relationships with the audience involves active engagement and fostering two-way communication. Engaging content, responding to feedback, and addressing concerns or inquiries contribute to a positive brand-consumer relationship. Brands that engage authentically and transparently, like Wendy's on Twitter with its witty and humorous responses, build stronger connections.

8) **Evolving and Adapting to Market Trends:**

Brand building is an ongoing process that requires adaptation to evolving market trends and consumer preferences. Staying relevant means continuously innovating, updating strategies, and embracing change. Brands that evolve while staying true to their core values maintain their relevance and appeal. Adidas, for example, consistently adapts to trends by collaborating with influencers and releasing limited-edition collections.

9) **Measuring and Analyzing Brand Performance:**
   Assessing brand performance through key metrics is essential for evaluating the effectiveness of brand-building efforts. Analyzing metrics like brand awareness, perception, loyalty, and market share provides insights into the brand's health and areas for improvement. Data-driven insights help refine strategies and optimize future initiatives.

10) **Sustaining and Nurturing Brand Equity:**
   Continuously nurturing brand equity involves preserving brand integrity, staying consistent, and reinforcing the brand's value proposition. Sustained efforts to maintain a positive brand image, innovate, and exceed customer expectations ensure long-term success. Brands like Google consistently reinforce their brand equity through innovation, reliability, and user-centric products.

1.5 Impact of Brands:

The impact of brands is profound and far-reaching, influencing consumer behavior, perceptions, and the marketplace at large. Brands wield significant power in shaping consumer preferences and purchasing decisions. They create differentiation and evoke emotions, influencing how individuals perceive and interact with products or services. Strong brands engender trust, loyalty, and advocacy, fostering enduring relationships with consumers. They contribute to a company's value, driving financial success and market leadership. Beyond financial implications, brands often transcend mere products, becoming cultural icons or symbols of societal values. They establish benchmarks for quality, innovation, and customer experience, setting industry standards. Additionally, brands can have social, environmental, and ethical impacts, influencing consumer behaviors toward sustainability or social responsibility. Ultimately, the impact of brands extends well beyond the tangible market realm, permeating societal, cultural, and individual spheres, shaping perceptions, behaviors, and aspirations.

1.5.1 Impacts of Brands on Markets:

Following are the impacts of brand on market:

1) **Market Differentiation:**
   Brands play a pivotal role in market differentiation by offering unique value propositions and establishing distinctive identities. Strong brands create a competitive advantage by setting themselves apart from competitors. Through effective branding strategies encompassing unique messaging, visual identity, and customer experience, brands carve out their niche in the market. This differentiation influences consumer perceptions, preferences, and purchasing decisions, contributing significantly to market diversity and healthy competition.

2) **Consumer Behavior and Perception:**

Brands exert a profound influence on consumer behavior and perception within markets. They shape how consumers perceive the quality, reliability, and value of products or services. Positive brand associations foster trust and loyalty, influencing consumer preferences and purchase decisions. Additionally, strong brands often command premium pricing, illustrating their impact on perceived value and willingness to pay among consumers.

3) **Market Dynamics and Competition:**

Brands significantly impact market dynamics by influencing competition. Established brands with strong market presence create barriers to entry for new competitors. Their market dominance and brand loyalty can pose challenges for new entrants trying to gain traction. Moreover, brands often set benchmarks for industry standards, encouraging innovation and driving competition to meet or surpass these standards.

4) **Brand Loyalty and Customer Retention:**

The strength of a brand influences customer loyalty and retention rates within markets. Brands that successfully build trust, deliver consistent quality, and engage with consumers foster loyal customer bases. This loyalty translates into repeat purchases, reduced customer churn, and increased customer lifetime value. Strong brand loyalty enhances a brand's market share and stability within the industry.

5) **Market Segmentation and Targeting:**

Effective branding facilitates market segmentation and targeting strategies. Brands tailor their messaging, products, and experiences to specific consumer segments, aligning with their preferences, values, and aspirations. Through brand positioning and communication strategies, brands attract and resonate with target audiences, enabling more efficient and effective market penetration.

6) **Influence on Pricing Strategies:**

Brands wield influence over pricing strategies within markets. A strong brand image and perceived value allow brands to command premium prices compared to generic or lesser-known alternatives. Consumers often associate higher prices with superior quality or status, enabling brands to implement premium pricing strategies and maintain profitability.

7) **Market Share and Revenue Generation:**

Successful brands hold substantial market share, contributing significantly to revenue generation within their respective markets. They capitalize on their brand equity, market presence, and customer loyalty to capture a significant portion of consumer spending. Brands that effectively capture market share often become market leaders, influencing industry trends and directions.

8) **Market Expansion and Global Reach:**
Strong brands expand markets and venture into global territories. Well-established brands with a strong identity and global appeal can penetrate new markets with relative ease. The reputation and recognition they have built in their home markets serve as a launching pad for successful expansion strategies into new regions, contributing to the globalization of markets.

9) **Innovation and Market Evolution:**
Brands drive innovation and market evolution by setting benchmarks for quality, service, and customer experience. Market-leading brands continually innovate to maintain their competitive edge, pushing boundaries and driving industry standards. Their innovation often leads to market evolution, influencing how products or services are developed, delivered, and perceived by consumers.

10) **Impact on Industry Practices and Regulations:**
Influential brands can impact industry practices and regulations. They often advocate for changes in industry standards, environmental practices, or ethical guidelines. Through their influence and market clout, brands can drive shifts towards more sustainable, socially responsible, or consumer-friendly industry practices, setting precedents and shaping the regulatory landscape.

1.5.2 Impacts of Brands on Society:

Following are the impacts of brand on society:

1) **Cultural Influence and Identity Formation:**
Brands play a significant role in shaping cultural norms, values, and identities within societies. They contribute to shaping popular culture, influencing trends, lifestyles, and societal aspirations. Iconic brands often become symbols representing certain cultures or societal movements, contributing to the formation of cultural identities. For instance, brands like Coca-Cola or McDonald's are not just products but symbols of American culture, transcending geographical boundaries and influencing global cultures.

2) **Consumer Behavior and Lifestyle Choices:**
Brands significantly impact consumer behavior and lifestyle choices in society. They create desires, aspirations, and preferences through their marketing strategies and brand positioning. Consumers often identify with brands that align with their values, beliefs, and lifestyles. Brand associations influence consumer choices, from fashion preferences to the consumption of specific goods or services, shaping societal trends and consumption patterns.

3) **Brand Advocacy and Social Causes:**
Many brands actively engage in social causes, advocating for societal changes or supporting various social, environmental, or humanitarian initiatives. Brands

leverage their influence and reach to raise awareness, mobilize support, and drive positive change in society. For example, brands like Patagonia or TOMS Shoes are recognized for their commitment to environmental sustainability and social responsibility, inspiring consumers and industry peers alike.

4) **Economic Impact and Employment:**
Brands have a significant economic impact on society, contributing to job creation, economic growth, and market expansion. Successful brands generate revenue streams, create employment opportunities, and contribute to the overall economic health of societies. They support supply chains, stimulate local economies, and contribute to tax revenues, fostering economic development.

5) **Education and Information Dissemination:**
Brands often serve as vehicles for disseminating information and educating the public. They communicate messages, raise awareness, and provide information about products, services, or social issues. Brands with a strong presence and visibility utilize their platforms to educate consumers, promote awareness campaigns, or share important messages, contributing to public discourse and awareness.

6) **Influence on Ethical and Cultural Values:**
Brands can influence societal ethical values and cultural perceptions. Through their marketing strategies and brand messaging, brands can impact societal perceptions on various issues such as gender roles, diversity, sustainability, and ethical consumption. Brands that champion ethical practices and cultural inclusivity can influence societal norms and encourage positive change.

7) **Media and Communication Platforms:**
Brands often utilize various media and communication platforms to reach audiences, shaping media landscapes and communication trends. They invest in advertising, sponsorships, and collaborations, influencing content creation and media consumption habits. Brands leverage these platforms to communicate messages, entertain, and engage with audiences, contributing to the evolution of media and communication channels.

8) **Health and Well-being Impact:**
Brands, particularly in the healthcare and wellness sectors, have a substantial impact on public health and well-being. They promote healthy lifestyles, wellness practices, and healthcare products. Brands in these industries play a role in educating consumers, promoting healthy behaviors, and providing access to products or services that enhance well-being.

9) **Technology and Innovation Influence:**
Technological brands and innovators significantly impact societal progress and technological advancement. Brands in the tech industry drive innovation, shape technological landscapes, and influence societal behaviors. They introduce new

technologies, transform industries, and impacts how people live, work, communicate, and interact with technology, shaping societal norms and behaviors.

10) Civic Engagement and Public Discourse:

Brands often engage in societal issues, fostering civic engagement and public discourse. They use their platforms to voice opinions, address societal concerns, and encourage public dialogue on various topics. Brands that take a stance on social, political, or environmental issues can influence public perceptions, drive conversations, and inspire action within society.

1.5.3 Impacts of Brands on Business:

Following are the impacts of brand on business:

1) **Revenue Generation and Market Positioning:**

   Brands significantly impact a business's revenue generation capabilities and market positioning. Strong brands command premium prices, enhance customer loyalty, and drive repeat purchases, leading to increased sales and revenue. Furthermore, a well-established brand helps a business carve out a distinct market position, enabling it to differentiate itself from competitors and capture a larger share of the market.

2) **Customer Loyalty and Retention:**

   Brands contribute to building customer loyalty and retention, crucial factors for business success. A strong brand fosters emotional connections with consumers, leading to increased trust and loyalty. This loyalty translates into repeat business, reduced customer churn, and a stable customer base. Businesses with strong brands benefit from higher customer lifetime value and reduced marketing costs associated with acquiring new customers.

3) **Brand Equity and Financial Value:**

   Brands significantly impact a business's overall financial value and brand equity. Brand equity represents the perceived value and strength of a brand in the market. A brand with high equity commands greater consumer preference and willingness to pay a premium for its products or services. Additionally, strong brand equity positively influences a business's financial performance, attracting investors, and enhancing the company's valuation.

4) **Competitive Edge and Market Share:**

   Brands provide businesses with a competitive edge by creating differentiation and influencing consumer choices. A strong brand enhances a business's market share by capturing the attention and loyalty of consumers. It enables companies to withstand competition, maintain market leadership, and respond effectively to market changes. Brands that consistently deliver superior value and experiences gain a larger share of the market.

5) Risk Mitigation and Brand Resilience:

Strong brands offer businesses resilience against market fluctuations and crises. Brands with a solid reputation and established trust among consumers are more resilient during economic downturns or crises. They retain customer loyalty and confidence, mitigating potential risks and minimizing the impact of adverse situations. Effective brand management and a positive brand image act as a buffer, safeguarding businesses against uncertainties.

6) Employee Engagement and Brand Advocacy:

Brands influence employee engagement and advocacy within a business. Employees aligned with a brand's values and mission become brand advocates, driving positive brand experiences. Engaged employees are motivated to deliver exceptional customer service, embody the brand's ethos, and contribute to a positive brand image. Brand-aligned employees become ambassadors, positively impacting the brand both internally and externally.

7) Innovation and Market Adaptability:

Brands stimulate innovation and market adaptability within businesses. Strong brands encourage a culture of innovation, driving businesses to continuously improve products, services, and processes to meet evolving consumer needs. They provide businesses with the flexibility to adapt to changing market conditions, stay relevant, and lead in innovation within their respective industries.

8) Customer Acquisition and Brand Extensions:

Brands play a pivotal role in attracting new customers and facilitating brand extensions. A strong brand attracts new customers by leveraging its reputation, visibility, and positive word-of-mouth. Moreover, established brands can successfully extend their product lines or venture into new markets with lower perceived risk due to existing brand equity and consumer trust.

9) Brand Partnerships and Alliances:

Brands facilitate partnerships and alliances, enabling businesses to expand their reach and tap into new markets. Collaboration between strong brands can lead to mutually beneficial alliances, leveraging each other's strengths and customer bases. Co-branding or strategic alliances allow businesses to access new audiences and create synergistic value propositions, fostering growth and market expansion.

10) Strategic Decision Making and Long-term Growth:

Brands influence strategic decision-making and contribute to a business's long-term growth trajectory. A well-defined brand strategy guides business decisions, ensuring alignment with brand values and objectives. Brands provide a roadmap for sustained growth by guiding investments, expansions, and innovations, driving businesses towards long-term success and sustainability.

1.6 Branding Challenge & Opportunities:

Branding presents both challenges and opportunities in the dynamic landscape of business and marketing. The challenge lies in establishing a distinct identity and resonance amidst fierce competition, evolving consumer preferences, and rapidly changing market trends. Balancing consistency while adapting to new technologies, consumer behaviors, and societal shifts poses a challenge. However, within these challenges lie numerous opportunities. Brands can leverage technology for deeper consumer engagement, utilize data for personalized experiences, and tap into global markets for expansion. Embracing sustainability, social responsibility, and authentic storytelling can create deeper connections with consumers. Navigating these challenges effectively opens doors to innovation, differentiation, and a stronger emotional bond with audiences, ultimately leading to sustained growth and relevance in the market.

1.6.1 Branding Challenges:

Following are the branding challenges:

1) **Market Saturation and Competition:**
   The ever-expanding market and increasing competition present a significant challenge for brands. In saturated markets, standing out becomes daunting. Establishing a unique identity, differentiating from competitors, and capturing consumers' attention amidst numerous options pose substantial hurdles.
2) **Consistency Across Channels:**
   Maintaining consistent brand messaging, image, and experience across various channels and touchpoints is a challenge, especially in the era of omnichannel marketing. Ensuring uniformity in the digital space, social media, traditional advertising, and in-person interactions demands meticulous planning and execution.
3) **Adapting to Consumer Behavior Shifts:**
   Rapid shifts in consumer behavior, preferences, and expectations require brands to stay agile. Adapting to these changes in real-time while consistently meeting consumer demands without diluting brand identity is a considerable challenge.
4) **Technology and Digital Transformation:**
   Embracing and effectively utilizing emerging technologies and digital platforms pose challenges for brands. Integrating technological advancements such as AI, AR/VR, or data analytics to enhance consumer experiences while staying ahead of technological obsolescence demands continuous innovation and investment.
5) **Building Brand Trust and Credibility:**
   Establishing and maintaining trust amidst an era of skepticism and information overload is challenging. Ensuring transparency, delivering on promises, and managing public perceptions in the face of public scrutiny or negative feedback is crucial yet demanding.

6) **Globalization and Cultural Sensitivity:**
Expanding into global markets while navigating diverse cultures, languages, and societal norms presents challenges. Brands must strike a balance between global consistency and local relevance, ensuring their messaging and offerings resonate with diverse audiences without causing cultural misinterpretations or controversies.

7) **Sustainability and Social Responsibility:**
Consumers increasingly expect brands to champion sustainability and social responsibility. Balancing profitability with ethical practices, environmental consciousness, and social initiatives poses a challenge. Meeting these expectations while staying competitive in cost and quality requires strategic planning and commitment.

8) **Crisis Management and Reputation Risks:**
Managing crises, negative publicity, or brand reputation risks is a continuous challenge. Responding effectively to PR crises, addressing consumer concerns, and mitigating reputational damages demands swift action and effective communication strategies.

9) **Balancing Innovation and Tradition:**
Striking a balance between innovation and maintaining core brand values or traditions is challenging. Innovating to meet evolving consumer needs while preserving brand authenticity and heritage requires careful navigation.

10) **Measuring Brand Success and ROI:**
Measuring the success and return on investment (ROI) of branding initiatives remains a challenge. Quantifying the impact of branding efforts on revenue, market share, customer loyalty, and brand equity is complex and requires sophisticated metrics and analytics.

1.6.2 Branding Opportunities:

Following are the branding opportunities:

1) **Technological Advancements:**
Rapid technological advancements present brands with immense opportunities to innovate and enhance consumer experiences. Embracing emerging technologies like artificial intelligence (AI), augmented reality (AR), or data analytics allows brands to create personalized, immersive, and engaging experiences for consumers. Leveraging these tools can streamline operations, optimize marketing strategies, and offer unique value propositions, fostering stronger brand-consumer relationships.

2) **Global Market Expansion:**
With globalization, brands have unprecedented opportunities to expand into new markets and reach diverse audiences worldwide. Access to global markets through

e-commerce, digital platforms, and cross-border collaborations enables brands to tap into new consumer segments, adapt their offerings to local preferences, and establish a global footprint.

3) **Personalization and Consumer Engagement:**
Brands can leverage data analytics and consumer insights to personalize experiences and engage with consumers on a deeper level. Tailoring products, services, and marketing messages to individual preferences and behaviors enhances customer satisfaction, fosters loyalty, and drives repeat purchases.

4) **Sustainability and Social Responsibility:**
Embracing sustainability and social responsibility presents brands with opportunities to differentiate themselves and resonate with socially conscious consumers. Brands that adopt ethical practices, champion environmental causes, and integrate sustainability into their operations can attract a growing segment of consumers seeking purpose-driven and eco-friendly products/services.

5) **Omnichannel Strategies:**
Brands can leverage omnichannel strategies to provide seamless and integrated experiences across various touchpoints. Connecting physical stores with online platforms, social media, mobile apps, and other channels allows brands to create cohesive customer journeys, enhance convenience, and increase brand visibility and accessibility.

6) **Content Creation and Storytelling:**
Brands have the opportunity to harness the power of compelling storytelling and content creation. Engaging narratives that align with brand values and resonate with consumers' emotions can create lasting impressions, build brand affinity, and drive brand loyalty.

7) **Brand Partnerships and Collaborations:**
Collaborations with complementary brands or influencers offer opportunities to expand reach and tap into new audiences. Strategic partnerships can create synergies, amplify brand visibility, and introduce innovative offerings that cater to shared consumer segments.

8) **Employee Advocacy and Brand Ambassadors:**
Engaged employees can serve as brand advocates, promoting the brand's values and mission. Investing in employee engagement, training, and empowerment cultivates a workforce that embodies the brand's ethos, positively impacting customer interactions and brand perception.

9) **Data-Driven Decision Making:**
Harnessing the power of data analytics enables brands to make informed decisions. Analyzing consumer behavior, market trends, and performance metrics allows brands to optimize strategies, identify new opportunities, and fine-tune their offerings for maximum impact.

10) Customer Experience Enhancement:

Brands can differentiate themselves by prioritizing exceptional customer experiences. Emphasizing convenience, personalization, responsiveness, and after-sales service creates memorable experiences that foster customer loyalty and advocacy.

1.7 Essential Brand Components:

Essential brand components encompass a set of fundamental elements crucial for establishing a robust brand identity and resonance. These components include the brand's visual elements such as logos, color palettes, typography, and imagery, which serve as the visual cues representing the brand's personality and values. Additionally, the brand's verbal elements, including the brand name, tagline, slogans, and messaging, encapsulate the essence and promise of the brand, communicating its unique value proposition to consumers.

1) **Brand Identity:**

   Brand identity encompasses the visual elements that represent a brand, such as logos, colors, typography, and design styles. It's the face of the brand and serves as a visual cue for consumers to recognize and remember. A well-crafted brand identity ensures consistency across all brand touchpoints, reinforcing brand recall and fostering a strong visual connection with the audience. Notably, the Nike swoosh or Apple's minimalist design exemplify powerful and recognizable brand identities.

2) **Brand Name:**

   The brand name is a crucial component that embodies the brand's essence and sets the tone for consumer perception. It's the first impression and often the most enduring aspect of a brand. A strong brand name is memorable, easy to pronounce, and relevant to the brand's values and offerings. Companies like Google, with its distinctive and playful name, or Tesla, paying homage to inventor Nikola Tesla, have successfully crafted impactful brand names.

3) **Brand Positioning:**

   Brand positioning defines how a brand distinguishes itself in the minds of consumers relative to competitors. It involves identifying and communicating the brand's unique value proposition, target audience, and market niche. Effective brand positioning ensures that consumers perceive the brand favorably and distinctly. Volvo, for instance, positions itself as a brand synonymous with safety, setting itself apart in the automobile industry.

4) **Brand Storytelling:**

   Brand storytelling is a powerful tool for engaging consumers emotionally and creating a deeper connection. It involves narrating the brand's journey, values, and purpose in a compelling and relatable manner. A well-crafted brand story evokes emotions, builds trust, and humanizes the brand. Companies like Airbnb, sharing stories of hosts and guests, or Patagonia, emphasizing environmental activism, excel in impactful brand storytelling.

5) **Brand Values:**

Brand values represent the core beliefs and principles that guide a brand's actions and decisions. These values shape the brand's culture, behavior, and relationships with consumers. Brands that authentically embody and communicate their values resonate better with consumers who share similar beliefs. For example, Ben & Jerry's commitment to social responsibility and activism aligns with its brand values, attracting socially conscious consumers.

6) **Brand Voice and Tone:**

Brand voice and tone encompass the communication style and language used by the brand across various channels. Consistency in the brand's voice and tone helps in creating a cohesive and recognizable brand personality. Whether it's friendly, authoritative, playful, or formal, maintaining a consistent voice ensures that the brand's message remains coherent and recognizable. The distinct and playful tone of brands like Innocent Drinks resonates with their audience.

7) **Brand Promise:**

The brand promise is a commitment made by the brand to its consumers regarding the benefits and experiences they can expect. It sets expectations and forms the basis for trust and credibility. Delivering on the brand promise consistently strengthens consumer loyalty and advocacy. FedEx, with its promise of reliable and timely delivery, has built a brand known for its commitment to service.

8) **Brand Experience:**

Brand experience encompasses every interaction consumers have with the brand, including products, services, customer support, and overall engagement. Consistently delivering a positive and memorable brand experience reinforces brand loyalty and advocacy. Brands like Disney excel in providing immersive and magical experiences, creating lasting memories for their customers.

9) **Brand Differentiation:**

Brand differentiation highlights what sets a brand apart from competitors. It focuses on communicating unique features, benefits, or values that make the brand distinctive and desirable. Effective differentiation ensures that consumers perceive the brand as superior or preferable compared to alternatives. Brands like Airbnb, offering unique travel experiences, differentiate themselves from traditional lodging options.

10) **Brand Consistency:**

Brand consistency ties all components together, ensuring coherence and reliability across all brand interactions. Consistency in messaging, visuals, and experiences reinforces brand identity, builds trust and fosters a strong brand image. Brands that maintain consistency, such as Coca-Cola with its timeless logo and messaging, establish enduring connections with consumers.

1.8 Importance of Consumer Perception & Behaviour in Branding:

Consumer perception and behavior play a pivotal role in the success and effectiveness of branding strategies. Understanding and influencing how consumers perceive a brand and their subsequent behaviors are paramount for brand success. Consumer perception, shaped by brand messaging, experiences, and interactions, forms the basis of how individuals perceive a brand's identity, value, and relevance in their lives. It influences their decision-making process, purchase intentions, and loyalty towards a brand. Moreover, consumer behavior, influenced by perceptions, social factors, emotions, and past experiences, dictates how individuals interact with brands, engage with their products/services, and advocate for or against them. Brands that prioritize understanding consumer perceptions and behaviors can tailor their strategies to resonate with their target audience, foster emotional connections, address pain points, and fulfill evolving needs, ultimately creating stronger brand-consumer relationships and driving long-term brand success in the market.

1.8.1 Importance of Consumer Perception in Branding:

The multifaceted importance of consumer perception in branding, showcasing how it influences various aspects crucial for a brand's success in the market.

1) **Brand Image Formation:**

   Consumer perception plays a pivotal role in shaping a brand's image. It's the lens through which individuals view a brand, influenced by their experiences, emotions, and interactions. This perception forms the foundation of how consumers relate to and differentiate between brands. For instance, a brand known for reliability and quality will be perceived differently from one associated with affordability or innovation. Companies strive to shape this perception through consistent messaging, product quality, customer service, and overall brand experience.

2) **Building Trust and Loyalty:**

   Consumer perception heavily impacts trust and loyalty towards a brand. When consumers perceive a brand positively, trust follows suit. Trust is the cornerstone of a long-term relationship between a brand and its customers. Consumers tend to remain loyal to brands they trust, leading to repeat purchases and advocacy. Therefore, fostering a positive perception is crucial for brands aiming to cultivate loyalty among their customer base.

3) **Competitive Edge:**

   In a competitive market, consumer perception can serve as a differentiator. Brands with a favorable perception often stand out amidst their competitors. A positive perception can act as a competitive advantage, influencing consumers to choose one brand over another. This edge can be leveraged through effective branding strategies that highlight unique selling propositions and resonate with consumers' values and preferences.

4) **Brand Equity and Value:**

Consumer perception contributes significantly to a brand's equity and overall value. Brands perceived positively command higher value in the market. A strong brand with a positive perception can charge premium prices compared to its competitors. This perception-driven value extends beyond tangible assets, encompassing consumer sentiment, brand recognition, and the overall goodwill associated with the brand.

5) **Influence on Purchase Decisions:**

The way consumers perceive a brand directly impacts their purchasing decisions. Positive perceptions often lead to a higher inclination to buy a product or service. A brand that is perceived as reliable, trustworthy, and aligned with consumer values tends to attract more customers. This perception influences the consumer's willingness to pay and their likelihood of choosing one brand over another when making a purchase.

6) **Market Positioning and Target Audience:**

Understanding consumer perception aids in effective market positioning. Brands analyze consumer perceptions to identify their target audience accurately. By aligning their messaging, products, and services with the desired perception of their target audience, brands can position themselves strategically in the market. This alignment ensures that the brand resonates with the right consumers, thereby enhancing its market presence.

7) **Adaptation and Innovation:**

Consumer perception serves as a valuable feedback mechanism for brands. It provides insights into consumer preferences, needs, and evolving trends. Brands that actively listen and adapt to changing perceptions can innovate their products or services to better cater to consumer demands. This adaptability and innovation reinforce a positive brand image and maintain relevance in a dynamic market.

8) **Crisis Management and Reputation:**

During times of crisis or negative publicity, consumer perception can make or break a brand. Brands with a strong positive perception often weather crises better than those with weaker perceptions. A positive perception built on trust and goodwill can mitigate the impact of negative events. Brands that handle crises transparently and effectively can even turn around negative perceptions, rebuilding trust and preserving their reputation.

9) **Emotional Connection and Brand Advocacy:**

Consumer perception isn't solely rational; it's deeply tied to emotions. Brands that evoke positive emotions and resonate with consumers on an emotional level tend to create stronger connections. These emotional connections lead to brand advocacy, where satisfied customers become brand ambassadors, spreading positive perceptions through word-of-mouth and social media, amplifying the brand's reach and impact.

10) **Long-Term Sustainability and Growth:**

Ultimately, consumer perception is integral to a brand's long-term sustainability and growth. Brands that consistently manage and shape their perception positively create a solid foundation for sustained success. By nurturing a positive perception, brands can maintain relevance, adapt to changing market dynamics, and foster growth opportunities, ensuring their sustainability in the long run.

1.8.2 Importance of Consumer Behaviour in Branding:

Consumer behavior plays a pivotal role in shaping the branding strategies of businesses.

1) **Understanding Consumer Needs and Preferences:**

Consumer behavior analysis helps brands comprehend the needs, preferences, and motivations of their target audience. By delving into consumer behavior patterns, businesses can discern what drives consumers to make purchasing decisions. Understanding these drivers allows brands to tailor their products, services, and marketing strategies to better align with consumer desires and preferences, ensuring a more effective and targeted approach.

2) **Segmentation and Targeting:**

Consumer behavior insights enable brands to segment their market effectively. By categorizing consumers based on behavior, demographics, psychographics, and purchasing habits, brands can identify specific segments to target. This segmentation allows for tailored marketing strategies, messaging, and product offerings, ensuring a more personalized approach that resonates with each segment's unique preferences and behaviors.

3) **Product Development and Innovation:**

Consumer behavior research provides valuable insights for product development and innovation. By understanding what consumers want, what problems they face, and what improvements they seek, brands can create products that better meet consumer needs. This understanding fosters innovation by enabling businesses to develop solutions that address specific pain points or offer unique features that align with consumer preferences.

4) **Building Brand Personality and Identity:**
Consumer behavior influences how brands shape their identity and personality. Brands that align their image, messaging, and values with the behaviors and attitudes of their target audience can establish a more authentic and relatable brand persona. Understanding consumer behavior allows brands to craft a consistent and appealing brand image that resonates with their audience, fostering stronger connections and loyalty.

5) **Effective Communication and Messaging:**
Analyzing consumer behavior aids in crafting more impactful communication and messaging strategies. Understanding how consumers consume information, their preferred communication channels, and the language that resonates with them helps brands create compelling and relevant marketing campaigns. By speaking the language of their audience and delivering messages that align with their behavior, brands can engage consumers more effectively.

6) **Influencing Purchase Decisions:**
Consumer behavior heavily influences purchase decisions. Understanding the decision-making process, factors influencing purchase behavior, and the buyer's journey allows brands to influence these decisions more effectively. By addressing consumer concerns, providing relevant information, and leveraging psychological triggers, brands can positively impact the decision-making process and increase the likelihood of conversions.

7) **Customer Experience Enhancement:**
Consumer behavior insights are instrumental in enhancing the overall customer experience. By understanding how consumers interact with products, services, and touchpoints, brands can optimize these experiences. This optimization spans across various aspects, including user interface design, customer service interactions, post-purchase support, and overall brand interactions, ensuring a seamless and satisfying customer journey.

8) **Predictive Analysis and Forecasting:**
Analyzing consumer behavior patterns allows brands to predict future trends and make informed business decisions. By leveraging data analytics and consumer behavior insights, businesses can forecast market trends, anticipate shifts in consumer preferences, and adapt their strategies accordingly. This proactive approach enables brands to stay ahead of the curve and capitalize on emerging opportunities.

9) **Brand Loyalty and Advocacy:**
Understanding consumer behavior is instrumental in fostering brand loyalty and advocacy. By identifying what drives loyalty, whether it's superior product quality, exceptional customer service, or emotional connections, brands can cultivate stronger relationships with their customers. Satisfied and loyal customers often

become brand advocates, recommending products or services to others, thereby positively influencing brand perception.

10) Continuous Improvement and Adaptation:

Consumer behavior analysis is an ongoing process that facilitates continuous improvement and adaptation. Markets evolve, and consumer preferences change over time. Brands that consistently monitor and analyze consumer behavior can adapt their strategies, innovate, and refine their offerings to stay relevant and maintain a competitive edge in the ever-changing landscape.

❖❖❖❖❖

Multiple Choice Questions

1) **------------ is the process of creating and managing a distinctive identity for a product or service.**
   a) Innovation b) Branding c) Hoarding d) Neglect
2) **------------ are unique characteristics that distinguish a brand and contribute to its recognition.**
   a) Collaboration b) Features c) Ignorance d) Arbitration
3) **------------ involves outlining strategies to establish and maintain a brand's identity.**
   a) Hoarding b) Brand Planning c) Exploitation d) Innovation
4) **------------ are the visual and auditory components that contribute to brand recognition.**
   a) Communication b) Brand Elements c) Arbitration d) Hoarding
5) **The ------------ involves various stages such as brand positioning, targeting, and messaging.**
   a) Neglect b) Brand Building Process
   c) Collaboration d) Ignorance
6) **The ------------ of brands extends beyond markets to influence society and business.**
   a) Exploitation b) Impact c) Hoarding d) Innovation
7) **Branding challenges and opportunities arise from the need to ------------ and adapt to market trends.**
   a) Ignorance b) Arbitration c) Innovate d) Hoard
8) **Essential brand components include brand ------------ identity, and positioning.**
   a) Collaboration b) Hoarding c) Elements d) Exploitation
9) **The importance of consumer perception and behavior in branding emphasizes the role of ------------ preferences.**
   a) Hoarding b) Arbitration c) Ignorance d) Consumer

10) ------------ is the emotional and psychological response a brand evokes in consumers.

a) Innovation b) Hoarding c) Ignorance d) Brand Image

11) Brand Planning involves developing a ------------ to guide brand development and marketing activities.

a) Hoarding b) Strategy c) Arbitration d) Ignorance

12) Brand elements, such as logos and slogans, contribute to a brand's ------------ recognition.

a) Collaboration b) Hoarding c) Exploitation d) Visual

13) Steps of the brand building process include ------------ messaging, and establishing brand loyalty.

a) Ignorance b) Collaboration c) Positioning d) Arbitration

14) The impact of brands on society includes shaping ------------ and influencing cultural norms.

a) Hoarding b) Innovation

c) Communication d) Identities

15) Branding challenges and opportunities arise from the need to ------------ to changing consumer preferences.

a) Ignorance b) Arbitration c) Innovate d) Hoard

16) Essential brand components include a consistent brand ------------ across various touchpoints.

a) Collaboration b) Hoarding c) Identity d) Exploitation

17) The importance of consumer perception and behavior in branding highlights the need for understanding ------------ preferences.

a) Hoarding b) Arbitration c) Ignorance d) Consumer

18) Brand Planning involves developing a ------------ to guide brand development and marketing activities.

a) Hoarding b) Strategy c) Arbitration d) Ignorance

19) Brand elements, such as logos and slogans, contribute to a brand's ------------ recognition.

a) Collaboration b) Hoarding c) Exploitation d) Visual

20) Steps of the brand building process include ------------ , messaging, and establishing brand loyalty.

a) Ignorance b) Collaboration c) Positioning d) Arbitration

21) The impact of brands on society includes shaping ------------ and influencing cultural norms.

a) Hoarding b) Innovation

c) Communication d) Identities

22) **Branding challenges and opportunities arise from the need to ------------ to changing consumer preferences.**

a) Ignorance b) Arbitration c) Innovate d) Hoard

23) **Essential brand components include a consistent brand ------------ across various touchpoints.**

a) Collaboration b) Hoarding c) Identity d) Exploitation

24) **The importance of consumer perception and behavior in branding highlights the need for understanding ------------ preferences.**

a) Hoarding b) Arbitration c) Ignorance d) Consumer

25) **Brand Planning involves developing a ------------ to guide brand development and marketing activities.**

a) Hoarding b) Strategy c) Arbitration d) Ignorance

Ans : **1)** b, **2)** b, **3)** b, **4)** b, **5)** b, **6)** b, **7)** c, **8)** c, **9)** d, **10)** d, **11)** b, **12)** a, **13)** c, **14)** c, **15)** c, **16)** c, **17)** d, **18)** b, **19)** c, **20)** c, **21)** d, **22)** c, **23)** c, **24)** d, **25)** b.

Review Questions

Q. 1. What is mean by Branding? State the Features of Branding.
Q. 2. Explain the Importance of Branding.
Q. 3. What is mean by Brand Planning? Explain the Process of Brand Planning.
Q. 4. Discuss in detail about Factors Influencing Brand Planning.
Q. 5. Explain Importance of Brand Planning.
Q. 6. What is mean by Brand Elements? Write Various Brand Elements.
Q. 7. Discuss about the Essential Brand Components.
Q. 8. Explain in detail Brand Building Process.
Q. 9. Explain the Impacts of Brands on Market.
Q.10. Write about the Impacts of Brands on Society.
Q.11. Explain in detail Impacts of Brands on Business.
Q.12. Discuss about the Branding Challenges and Opportunities.
Q.13. Explain the Importance of Consumer Perception in Branding.
Q.14. Explain the Importance of Consumer Behaviour in Branding.
Q.14. **Write Short Notes on following:**

- **a)** Features of Branding.
- **b)** Importance of Branding.
- **c)** Process of Brand Planning.
- **d)** Impacts of Brands on Market.
- **e)** Branding Challenges.
- **f)** Branding Opportunities.
- **g)** Consumer Behaviour and Branding

UNIT 2

Brand Building

Introduction:

Brand building encapsulates the strategic efforts and activities aimed at crafting a distinct identity, perception, and value proposition for a product, service, or organization. It involves establishing a unique personality, voice, and visual identity that resonates with the target audience, fostering trust, loyalty, and credibility. Through consistent messaging, storytelling, customer experiences, and the delivery of exceptional quality or services, brand building cultivates a strong emotional connection, positioning the brand as a preferred choice amidst competition. It's a continuous process that focuses on shaping perceptions, creating differentiation, and fostering meaningful relationships with consumers, ultimately driving affinity and long-term success.

2.1 Brand Building:

Brand building is the strategic process of crafting a unique and resonant identity for a product, service, or organization in the minds of consumers. It involves meticulously shaping perceptions, emotions, and experiences associated with the brand to create an enduring connection. Through a cohesive blend of purposeful messaging, consistent visual elements, compelling storytelling, and delivering on promises, brand building cultivates trust, loyalty, and recognition among its target audience. It goes beyond mere advertising, encompassing every interaction and touch point, aiming to create a distinctive impression that not only captures attention but also fosters a lasting and impactful relationship with consumers.

2.1.1 Meaning:

Brand building refers to the deliberate and strategic process of establishing and nurturing a distinctive identity for a product, service, or company. It involves meticulously cultivating a unique brand image through consistent messaging, visual elements, and customer experiences. By focusing on creating emotional connections, fostering trust, and consistently delivering value, brand building aims to carve out a meaningful and lasting space in consumers' minds. It extends beyond marketing efforts, encompassing every interaction, communication, and touch point, ultimately shaping perceptions, loyalty, and preference among the target audience.

2.1.2 Definitions:

Following are the definitions of Brand Building:

1) **Philip Kotler:**
   "Brand building is the process of creating a strong, favorable, and unique perception of a brand in the minds of consumers. It involves consistently delivering on promises, establishing emotional connections, and nurturing customer loyalty."
2) **David Aaker:**
   "Brand building is the deliberate and strategic effort to create and sustain brand equity. It involves developing and managing brand identity elements to differentiate a brand and shape consumer perceptions."
3) **Keller and Lehmann:**
   "Brand building is the process of managing a brand through carefully planned strategies to create a strong, favorable, and distinctive brand image, ensuring it remains relevant and meaningful to consumers."
4) **Jean-Noël Kapferer:**
   "Brand building is the strategic endeavor to create strong, emotional, and lasting relationships between a brand and its customers. It's about forging deep connections that go beyond functional benefits."

2.1.3 Importance of Brand Building:

Following are the importance of brand building:

1) **Recognition and Recall:**

Brand building is vital for establishing recognition and recall in the minds of consumers. A strong brand identity, comprising a unique logo, color palette, and consistent messaging, helps customers easily identify and remember your brand amidst a sea of competitors. This recognition is crucial in today's saturated market, where consumers are bombarded with numerous options. Brands like Coca-Cola or Nike have successfully ingrained their logos and brand elements into the global consumer psyche, ensuring instant recognition and recall.

2) **Trust and Credibility:**

A well-established brand instills trust and credibility among consumers. When a brand consistently delivers on its promises, maintains quality standards, and provides excellent customer service, it builds a positive reputation. This credibility fosters trust, encouraging customers to choose your brand over others. Trust is a cornerstone of brand loyalty, as consumers are more likely to remain loyal to a brand they trust, leading to repeat purchases and positive word-of-mouth referrals.

3) **Competitive Edge and Differentiation:**

Effective brand building sets you apart from competitors by highlighting your unique value proposition. It helps convey what makes your products or services distinct in the market. Whether its superior quality, innovative features, or exceptional customer experiences, a strong brand communicates why customers should choose you over competitors. Apple's branding, emphasizing innovation and sleek design, exemplifies how differentiation contributes to a competitive edge.

4) **Emotional Connection and Loyalty:**

Brands that evoke emotions create stronger connections with consumers. Emotional branding taps into customers' feelings, aspirations, and values, fostering a deep connection beyond product features. When customers feel emotionally connected to a brand, they become loyal advocates who not only buy products but also endorse and defend the brand. Companies like Dove have successfully leveraged emotional branding with their "Real Beauty" campaign, resonating with consumers on a personal level.

5) **Premium Pricing and Value Perception:**

A well-established brand often commands a premium price compared to generic or lesser-known alternatives. Effective branding elevates the perceived value of products or services, allowing companies to justify higher prices based on brand equity. Consumers are often willing to pay more for brands they perceive as higher quality, reliable, or aligned with their personal values. Brands like Rolex or Mercedes-Benz capitalize on their strong brand equity to maintain premium pricing.

6) **Consistency and Cohesion:**

Brand consistency across all touch points is essential for effective brand building. From advertising to customer service interactions, maintaining a consistent brand voice, visual identity, and messaging reinforces brand recall and reliability. Consistency builds trust and credibility while preventing confusion among consumers, ensuring a cohesive brand experience regardless of the platform or channel.

7) **Market Expansion and Adaptability:**
Strong branding facilitates market expansion and adaptability. A well-established brand can seamlessly introduce new products or enter different markets while leveraging its existing brand equity. This flexibility allows brands to evolve and stay relevant in dynamic market conditions. For instance, Google expanded its brand from a search engine to various products and services, leveraging its strong brand reputation.

8) **Employee Engagement and Advocacy:**
Brand building isn't limited to external audiences; it also impacts internal stakeholders. A strong brand with a compelling vision and values motivates employees, fostering a sense of pride and purpose. Engaged employees become brand ambassadors, positively influencing customer interactions and advocating for the brand, thereby enhancing the overall brand image.

9) **Long-Term Sustainability:**
Building a robust brand is an investment in long-term sustainability. A strong brand withstands market fluctuations and economic challenges better than weaker brands. It creates a buffer against short-term crises and helps maintain customer loyalty during challenging times. Brands like Coca-Cola and McDonald's have endured for decades due to their strong brand foundations.

10) **Brand Expansion and Diversification:**
Successful brand building opens opportunities for brand extensions and diversification. A trusted brand can explore new product categories or enter adjacent markets with relative ease, leveraging existing brand equity. For instance, Amazon expanded from an online bookstore to a diverse e-commerce giant, utilizing its strong brand reputation to venture into various industries.

2.1.4 Brand Building Strategies:

Brand building strategies encompass a range of approaches tailored to enhance a brand's visibility, credibility, and resonance with its target audience. Some key strategies include:

1) **Defining a Robust Brand Identity:**
Establishing a brand identity is foundational. It involves determining the core values, mission, and vision that your brand embodies. This identity serves as a guiding light for all brand-related decisions, from design elements to marketing strategies. For instance, Nike's brand identity revolves around athleticism, innovation, and empowerment, evident in its iconic tagline "Just Do It." A strong brand identity

ensures consistency in messaging, which resonates deeply with consumers, fostering trust and loyalty.

2) **Audience Understanding and Targeting:**

Understanding your audience is pivotal. Conduct thorough market research to comprehend your target demographics' preferences, behaviors, pain points, and aspirations. Airbnb, for instance, extensively studies its diverse audience to offer personalized experiences that cater to various traveler segments. Tailoring your brand messaging and offerings to align with your audience's needs and aspirations is essential for forging lasting connections.

3) **Consistent Branding Across Channels:**

Maintaining consistency in branding elements logo, color palette, typography, and tone is imperative. This uniformity across all touchpoints reinforces brand recall and builds credibility. Apple exemplifies this through its consistent minimalist design and messaging, ensuring a seamless and recognizable brand experience across products and marketing materials.

4) **Compelling and Varied Content Creation:**

Creating compelling content is essential to engage and retain your audience. This content, spanning blog posts, videos, infographics, and podcasts, should align with your brand's ethos and address your audience's interests. Red Bull's content strategy, centered on extreme sports and adventure, resonates with its audience of thrill-seekers, fostering a strong emotional connection and brand loyalty.

5) **Effective Digital Marketing Strategies:**

Embrace the digital landscape to reach a wider audience. Employing SEO tactics, leveraging social media platforms, deploying targeted email campaigns, and utilizing paid advertising channels are crucial for maximizing visibility, engagement, and conversions. Coca-Cola's innovative digital campaigns, such as personalized bottle labels and user-generated content, have amplified its reach and engagement.

6) **Prioritizing Exceptional Customer Experiences:**

Providing exceptional customer experiences at every interaction point is paramount. Customer-centricity builds brand loyalty and advocacy. Brands like Zappos have built a reputation by prioritizing customer service, fostering a loyal customer base that appreciates the brand's commitment to satisfaction.

7) **Emotionally Resonant Storytelling:**

Crafting authentic and emotionally resonant brand stories creates a deeper connection with consumers. Brands like Dove and their "Real Beauty" campaign evoke powerful emotions and promote inclusivity, resonating with audiences beyond mere product advertising, thereby fostering a sense of belonging.

8) **Strategic Collaborations and Partnerships:**

Collaborating with influencers, complementary brands, or industry leaders can significantly amplify brand visibility and credibility. For instance, Adidas partnering with artists, athletes, and influencers has expanded its reach and relevance among diverse consumer segments, staying culturally relevant.

9) **Continuous Monitoring and Adaptation:**

   Continuously analyzing consumer feedback, market trends, and competitor strategies is crucial for adaptation and evolution. Flexibility and agility allow brands to stay ahead in a dynamic market landscape, like how Netflix constantly adapts its content strategy based on user preferences and global trends.

10) **Community Engagement and Advocacy:**

    Building a community around your brand fosters a sense of belonging and loyalty. Engaging with your audience, encouraging user-generated content, and facilitating meaningful conversations create a community that not only advocates for the brand but also contributes to its growth. LEGO's engagement with its fan community through user-generated content and collaborative projects has led to increased brand advocacy and innovation.

2.2 The Impact of Advertising in Building Brand Equity:

Advertising plays a pivotal role in shaping brand equity by elevating brand visibility, fostering emotional connections, and reinforcing brand attributes. Through strategic messaging and visual storytelling, advertisements cultivate consumer perceptions, preferences, and loyalty towards a brand. Consistent and impactful advertising campaigns not only increase brand recall but also contribute to brand associations, trust, and resonance in the minds of consumers. Over time, effective advertising contributes significantly to enhancing brand equity, influencing purchase decisions, and maintaining a competitive edge in the market.

1) **Brand Awareness and Exposure:**

   Advertising plays a pivotal role in creating brand awareness and exposure. Through various channels like TV, radio, print, digital media, and social platforms, brands reach a wide audience, ensuring their presence is felt. Consistent and strategic advertising campaigns introduce the brand to potential customers, increasing its visibility and recognition. For instance, Coca-Cola's iconic Christmas ads or Nike's compelling commercials have contributed significantly to their brand recognition globally.

2) **Establishing Brand Image and Identity:**

   Advertising helps shape a brand's image and identity in consumers' minds. By crafting messages, visuals, and stories, advertising influences how consumers perceive the brand. Whether portraying luxury, reliability, innovation, or other brand attributes, consistent messaging and creative storytelling through advertising establish the desired brand image. Apple's advertising, emphasizing sleek design and user experience, has solidified its image as an innovative and premium brand.

3) **Building Brand Associations:**

Effective advertising helps create positive brand associations by linking the brand with specific values, emotions, or experiences. By strategically aligning the brand with certain traits or lifestyles, advertising influences consumers' perceptions and associations with the brand. For example, through its "Just Do It" campaign, Nike associated its brand with determination, empowerment, and athleticism, shaping consumer perceptions and building strong brand associations.

4) **Enhancing Brand Recall and Recognition:**

Advertising significantly contributes to improving brand recall and recognition. Consistent exposure to a brand through various advertising channels reinforces its presence in consumers' minds. Catchy slogans, jingles, or visual elements used in advertisements aid in recalling the brand when making purchasing decisions. McDonald's, with its iconic "I'm Lovin' It" jingle, has successfully increased brand recall among consumers.

5) **Creating Emotional Connections:**

Advertising is a powerful tool for establishing emotional connections between brands and consumers. Compelling storytelling, relatable narratives, or heartwarming campaigns evoke emotions, fostering deeper connections with the audience. Brands like Dove, through its "Real Beauty" campaign, have successfully connected with consumers on an emotional level, promoting inclusivity and self-acceptance.

6) **Differentiation and Competitive Edge:**

Advertising helps differentiate a brand from its competitors by highlighting its unique selling propositions. Communicating distinctive features, benefits, or values through advertising positions the brand uniquely in consumers' minds. Effective advertising campaigns showcase what sets the brand apart, giving it a competitive edge. For instance, in the smartphone market, Samsung's advertising often emphasizes product features and technological advancements, setting itself apart from competitors.

7) **Driving Sales and Revenue:**

Well-executed advertising campaigns have a direct impact on driving sales and revenue for a brand. By reaching out to potential customers and persuading them to make purchasing decisions, advertising influences consumer behavior. Calls-to-action in advertisements, limited-time offers, or promotional deals often prompt consumers to buy, contributing to increased sales and revenue generation for the brand.

8) **Continuous Brand Reinforcement:**

Advertising plays a crucial role in reinforcing the brand's message, values, and promises. Continuous exposure to consistent brand messaging through advertising ensures that the brand stays top-of-mind among consumers. This reinforcement is essential for maintaining brand loyalty and retaining existing customers while attracting new ones.

9) **Global Reach and Market Expansion:**

Advertising enables brands to reach a global audience, facilitating market expansion and international growth. Through various advertising mediums and campaigns tailored to different regions and cultures, brands can penetrate new markets and establish their presence worldwide. Companies like Coca-Cola or McDonald's have successfully expanded their global footprint through extensive and culturally sensitive advertising efforts.

10) **Long-Term Brand Equity Development:**

Ultimately, advertising contributes significantly to the long-term development of brand equity. Consistent, impactful, and strategic advertising efforts over time build brand equity by creating a strong brand identity, fostering consumer loyalty, and enhancing the brand's perceived value. Brands with well-established equity, nurtured through advertising, enjoy lasting customer relationships, resilience in market fluctuations, and sustained success.

2.3 Marketing Communications and Brand Building:

Marketing communications are the linchpin in brand building, serving as the conduit for conveying a brand's essence, values, and offerings to its audience. Through various channels like advertising, public relations, social media, and content creation, marketing communications craft a cohesive narrative that resonates with consumers. Consistent and engaging messaging not only amplifies brand visibility but also cultivates brand perceptions and loyalty. The alignment of marketing communications with the brand's identity and objectives ensures a unified and impactful brand presence, ultimately contributing to sustained brand building efforts.

1) **Consistent Messaging:**

Marketing communications play a pivotal role in delivering a consistent brand message across various channels. Consistency in messaging ensures that consumers receive a unified and coherent impression of the brand, reinforcing its identity and value proposition. Whether through advertising, social media, PR, or content marketing, maintaining consistent messaging strengthens brand recall and fosters trust among consumers.

2) **Brand Awareness and Exposure:**

Marketing communications serve as a vehicle for increasing brand awareness and exposure. By strategically utilizing different channels and mediums, brands reach a wider audience, introducing themselves and their offerings to potential customers. Consistent and targeted communication efforts ensure that the brand remains visible and top-of-mind among consumers, thereby enhancing its recognition and recall.

3) **Building Brand Image and Perception:**
Effective marketing communications contribute significantly to shaping the brand's image and perception in consumers' minds. Through storytelling, visuals, and compelling narratives, brands can influence how they are perceived by their target audience. Strategic communication efforts can position a brand as innovative, trustworthy, eco-friendly, or customer-centric, thereby shaping consumer perceptions and fostering positive brand associations.

4) **Establishing Emotional Connections:**
Marketing communications have the power to evoke emotions and create meaningful connections with consumers. Compelling storytelling, relatable narratives, and impactful campaigns can resonate deeply with the audience, eliciting emotions that foster brand loyalty and affinity. Brands like Dove, with their "Real Beauty" campaign, have successfully connected with consumers on an emotional level, building stronger and more enduring relationships.

5) **Differentiation and Competitive Edge:**
Marketing communications play a crucial role in highlighting a brand's unique selling propositions and differentiators. Through targeted messaging, brands can communicate what sets them apart from competitors, emphasizing their strengths and value propositions. Effective communication of these differentiators creates a competitive edge, influencing consumer choices and preferences in the market.

6) **Engagement and Relationship Building:**
Marketing communications facilitate engagement with consumers, fostering two-way communication and relationship building. Brands that actively engage with their audience through social media interactions, personalized communications, or interactive campaigns create a sense of community and belonging. Engaged consumers are more likely to develop brand loyalty and advocate for the brand among their peers.

7) **Consistency Across Channels:**
Effective marketing communications ensure consistency across various channels and touchpoints. Whether it's print, digital, social media, or in-person interactions, maintaining a cohesive brand voice, visual identity, and messaging strengthens brand equity. Consistency across channels reinforces brand recognition, builds credibility, and enhances the overall brand experience for consumers.

8) **Driving Sales and Conversion:**
Marketing communications directly influence consumer behavior by driving sales and conversions. Compelling calls-to-action, persuasive messaging, and targeted campaigns encourage consumers to take desired actions, such as making a purchase or signing up for a service. Well-executed marketing communications initiatives effectively guide consumers through the buyer's journey, ultimately impacting the bottom line.

9) **Adaptability and Innovation:**
Marketing communications strategies should be adaptable and innovative to stay relevant in a constantly evolving landscape. Brands that continuously innovate their communication approaches, embrace new technologies, and adapt to changing consumer behaviors are better positioned to maintain relevance and competitiveness. Being agile allows brands to capture emerging trends and engage with their audience effectively.

10) **Measuring and Optimizing Strategies:**
Effective marketing communications involve measuring the impact of strategies and optimizing them for better results. Metrics such as brand awareness, engagement rates, conversion rates, and customer feedback provide valuable insights. Analyzing these metrics helps in understanding what works best, enabling brands to refine their communication strategies for improved effectiveness and efficiency.

2.4 Growing and Sustaining Brands:

Growing and sustaining brands necessitates a continuous cycle of innovation, consumer engagement, and adaptation. Consistent delivery of quality products or services, coupled with responsive customer service, fosters brand loyalty. By staying attuned to market shifts, embracing consumer feedback, and evolving with changing trends, brands can remain relevant and retain consumer interest. Building a robust brand involves a perpetual commitment to innovation and maintaining relevance, ultimately enabling brands to grow and endure amidst dynamic market landscapes.

2.4.1 Growing Brands:

Following are the strategies for growing brands:

1) **Innovation and Product Development:**
Continuous innovation in product offerings is crucial for brand growth. Brands like Apple have sustained growth by consistently introducing innovative products that captivate consumers' interests and address evolving needs. This approach requires a keen understanding of market demands and technological advancements to stay ahead of the curve.

2) **Market Penetration Strategies:**
Expanding market reach through effective penetration strategies is vital. This can involve diversifying product lines, entering new geographic markets, or targeting untapped consumer segments. For instance, Coca-Cola penetrated emerging markets by adapting its product range to suit local tastes and preferences.

3) **Strategic Partnerships and Collaborations:**
Forming strategic partnerships can facilitate brand growth by leveraging the strengths of other brands or influencers. Collaborations can open new distribution

channels, introduce co-branded products, or increase brand exposure. Nike's collaborations with athletes and celebrities have significantly boosted its brand image and market presence.

4) **Customer-Centric Approach:**

Prioritizing customer needs and feedback is instrumental in brand growth. Brands that actively listen to customer preferences, engage in dialogue, and adapt offerings accordingly foster stronger relationships and build customer loyalty. Amazon's customer-centric approach, focused on convenience and service excellence, has been fundamental to its growth.

5) **Investment in Marketing and Advertising:**

Allocating resources to marketing and advertising initiatives is crucial for brand growth. Brands need to create compelling campaigns that resonate with their audience across various platforms. For example, Pepsi's strategic marketing campaigns, often aligned with pop culture, have contributed to its brand growth and visibility.

6) **Embrace Digital Transformation:**

Embracing digital platforms and technologies is essential in today's market. Brands should invest in e-commerce, social media, and digital marketing strategies to engage with consumers and stay relevant in a tech-savvy environment. Starbucks, for instance, has invested heavily in its mobile app and loyalty program, enhancing customer experience and driving growth.

7) **Consistent Branding and Positioning:**

Maintaining a consistent brand image and positioning reinforces consumer trust and recognition. Brands like Google have maintained a consistent brand identity across their products and services, contributing to sustained growth and a strong market position.

8) **Investment in Employee Training and Culture:**

A robust brand grows when employees embody its values and mission. Investing in employee training and fostering a positive work culture ensures consistent delivery of the brand promise. Companies like Zappos prioritize employee satisfaction, believing that happy employees lead to happy customers, contributing to brand growth.

9) **Data-Driven Decision Making:**

Leveraging data analytics enables brands to make informed decisions. Analyzing consumer behavior, market trends, and performance metrics allows for targeted strategies and optimizations. Companies like Netflix utilize data to personalize recommendations, enhancing the user experience and driving growth.

10) **Social Responsibility and Sustainability:**

Brands that demonstrate a commitment to social responsibility and sustainability often experience growth. Consumers are increasingly drawn to brands that align with their values. Patagonia's focus on sustainability and ethical practices has not only attracted environmentally conscious consumers but also contributed to its growth and brand loyalty.

2.4.2 Sustaining Brands:

Following are the strategies to sustain brands:

1) **Continuous Innovation:**
Sustaining a brand demands ongoing innovation to keep products or services fresh and aligned with evolving consumer needs. Brands like Tesla continuously innovate their electric vehicles, introducing new features and models to stay ahead in a competitive market. Innovation ensures that the brand remains relevant and appealing to its audience.

2) **Adaptation to Market Trends:**
Adapting to changing market trends and consumer preferences is crucial for sustained success. Brands must stay agile and flexible, adjusting their strategies and offerings accordingly. For instance, fast-food chains like McDonald's have adjusted their menus to cater to health-conscious consumers, ensuring sustained relevance.

3) **Brand Reinforcement through Communication:**
Consistent and strategic brand communication reinforces brand values and identity. Regularly reminding consumers about the brand's ethos and offerings through various channels, such as advertising, PR, and social media, strengthens brand recall and affinity. Coca-Cola's consistent messaging about happiness and togetherness is an example of effective brand reinforcement.

4) **Building Customer Relationships:**
Long-term sustainability relies on nurturing strong relationships with customers. Brands need to engage customers beyond transactions, offering personalized experiences and excellent customer service. Companies like Amazon prioritize customer satisfaction, building lasting relationships that drive sustained loyalty.

5) **Investment in Brand Experience:**
Providing a unique and memorable brand experience fosters sustained consumer interest and loyalty. Brands like Disney focus on creating immersive experiences, whether in theme parks or through their movies and merchandise, ensuring customers consistently return for the experience.

6) **Consistency in Quality:**
Maintaining consistent product or service quality is fundamental for brand sustainability. Consumers associate a brand with its quality standards, and any deviation can impact their trust. Brands like Apple are renowned for their high-quality products, ensuring sustained customer loyalty and positive perceptions.

7) **Strategic Partnerships and Collaborations:**
Forming alliances with other brands or influencers can inject fresh energy into a brand and reach new audiences. Collaborations allow brands to leverage each other's strengths and introduce innovative products or campaigns, contributing to sustained growth. Nike's collaborations with athletes and designers consistently excite its audience.

8) **Corporate Social Responsibility (CSR) Initiatives:**
Demonstrating a commitment to social causes and sustainability fosters positive brand perception and consumer trust. Brands engaging in meaningful CSR initiatives, like TOMS' one-for-one giving model, not only contribute to social causes but also sustain a positive brand image.

9) **Continuous Employee Engagement:**
Employees are brand ambassadors, and their engagement influences the brand's perception. Investing in employee well-being, training, and empowerment ensures they align with the brand's values, delivering consistent experiences. Brands like Google focus on creating a positive work culture, reflecting in their sustained brand success.

10) **Adaptability and Future Readiness:**
Brands must anticipate and prepare for future challenges and changes in the market. Remaining adaptable and forward-thinking allows brands to proactively navigate industry shifts, ensuring sustained relevance and success. Companies like Netflix consistently evolve their content strategies to adapt to changing entertainment consumption patterns.

2.5 Process Internal Branding:

Internal branding refers to the strategic cultivation of a brand-focused organizational culture among employees. It involves aligning the company's values, mission, and brand promise with the behaviors, attitudes, and actions of its workforce. By fostering a deep understanding of the brand's essence and goals within the organization, internal branding inspires employees to embody the brand's values, deliver consistent brand experiences, and become brand advocates. This alignment strengthens employee engagement, motivation, and commitment, ultimately enhancing the brand's external perception and customer experiences.

1) **Define Brand Values and Identity:**
The process of internal branding begins with clearly defining the brand's values, mission, and identity. Articulating the brand's core values, vision, and personality ensures a cohesive understanding among employees. This clarity forms the foundation for internal alignment and guides employees in embodying and advocating for the brand. For example, companies like Google or Disney have well-defined values that permeate their organizational culture.

2) **Communicate Brand Objectives and Goals:**
Transparent communication of brand objectives and goals is crucial for internal branding. Employees need to understand the brand's strategic direction, short-term goals, and long-term vision. Sharing these objectives fosters a sense of purpose and direction, aligning employees toward common goals. Clear communication ensures everyone is working towards achieving the same brand-centric objectives.

3) **Employee Engagement and Involvement:**
Engaging employees in the branding process is essential for internal alignment. Involving them in discussions, seeking their input, and valuing their perspectives create a sense of ownership and commitment to the brand. Companies often organize workshops, forums, or brainstorming sessions to encourage employee participation in shaping the brand's narrative and culture.

4) **Training and Development Programs:**
Implementing training and development programs centered on the brand's values and culture helps employees embody the brand. Training sessions on brand values, customer service standards, and brand storytelling empower employees to deliver consistent brand experiences. These programs equip employees with the necessary skills and knowledge to effectively represent the brand.

5) **Internal Brand Messaging and Storytelling:**
Crafting internal brand messaging and storytelling is pivotal for conveying the brand's essence to employees. Effective storytelling about the brand's history, achievements, and values creates an emotional connection and sense of pride among employees. Consistent messaging reinforces the brand's identity and fosters a shared understanding of what the brand stands for.

6) **Leadership Role in Brand Advocacy:**
Strong leadership commitment and advocacy are critical for successful internal branding. Leaders should exemplify the brand's values, embody its culture, and actively communicate and reinforce the brand's identity. When leadership demonstrates a genuine commitment to the brand, employees are more likely to embrace and emulate those values.

7) **Recognition and Reward Systems:**
Implementing recognition and reward systems that align with the brand's values reinforces desired behaviors and attitudes. Acknowledging and rewarding employees who exemplify the brand's values motivates others to follow suit. Recognizing employees for demonstrating brand-aligned behaviors reinforces the importance of the brand within the organization.

8) **Feedback Mechanisms and Listening Culture:**
Establishing feedback mechanisms fosters a culture of open communication and continuous improvement. Creating avenues for employees to provide feedback on the brand, culture, and internal processes encourages dialogue and demonstrates

that their opinions are valued. Actively listening to employee feedback helps in refining internal branding strategies and addressing potential gaps.

9) **Integration into Daily Operations:**

Embedding the brand into daily operations ensures consistent alignment with brand values. From customer interactions to decision-making processes, every aspect of operations should reflect the brand's values and culture. Integrating the brand into workflows and procedures reinforces its importance in shaping organizational behavior.

10) **Evaluation and Continuous Improvement:**

Regularly evaluating the effectiveness of internal branding initiatives is crucial for continuous improvement. Measuring employee engagement, brand understanding, and alignment with brand values helps in assessing the impact of internal branding efforts. Using these insights to refine strategies ensures ongoing alignment and improvement.

2.6 New Brand Launches:

Launching a new brand involves meticulous market research, strategic planning, brand identity development, compelling storytelling, coordinated marketing efforts, a successful launch event, post-launch engagement, continuous monitoring, scaling strategies, and long-term brand building. A well-executed launch sets the stage for the brand's success and growth in the market.

1) **Market Research and Analysis:**

Conducting thorough market research is the foundational step in launching a new brand. This involves analyzing the target market, identifying consumer needs, understanding competitors, and assessing market trends. Comprehensive research provides insights into consumer preferences, allowing for informed decisions regarding brand positioning, messaging, and strategies. Brands like Airbnb conducted extensive market research to identify gaps in the travel accommodation market before their launch.

2) **Defining Brand Strategy and Objectives:**

Establishing a clear brand strategy and setting objectives is crucial for a successful launch. Defining the brand's unique value proposition, positioning, and target audience ensures a focused approach. Clear objectives outline what the brand aims to achieve, whether it's market penetration, revenue targets, or brand awareness goals. This strategy forms the basis for all subsequent brand-building efforts during the launch phase.

3) **Developing Brand Identity and Visuals:**

Creating a compelling brand identity is pivotal for a successful launch. This involves designing a logo, color palette, typography, and visual elements that reflect the brand's personality and values. Consistent and impactful visuals help in establishing brand recognition and differentiation. For instance, the distinctive logo and visual identity of brands like Airbnb or Uber contributed significantly to their successful launches.

4) **Crafting Compelling Brand Story and Messaging:**
Building a compelling brand story and messaging is essential for connecting with consumers on an emotional level. Communicating the brand's narrative, values, and mission in a relatable and engaging manner creates a strong connection with the audience. A compelling story helps in generating interest, building anticipation, and attracting early adopters to the brand.

5) **Creating Marketing and Communication Plans:**
Developing comprehensive marketing and communication plans is crucial for reaching the target audience effectively. This involves choosing the right channels, such as social media, advertising, PR, content marketing, and influencer partnerships, to maximize visibility and engagement. Strategic planning ensures a coordinated and impactful launch campaign. Brands often utilize teaser campaigns or pre-launch activities to build anticipation and buzz, like Apple does before unveiling new products.

6) **Product or Service Launch:**
The actual launch of the product or service marks a critical moment in the brand launch process. Whether it's a physical product, an app, or a service, the launch event or release should align with the brand's messaging and positioning. A successful launch event generates excitement, garners media attention, and engages the target audience. Seamless execution during the launch phase is vital for making a strong first impression.

7) **Engagement and Relationship Building:**
Post-launch engagement with the audience is essential for sustaining momentum and building relationships. Interacting with early adopters, responding to feedback, and fostering a community around the brand helps in nurturing brand loyalty. Brands that actively engage with their audience through social media, events, or personalized interactions establish a loyal customer base.

8) **Continuous Monitoring and Adaptation:**
Monitoring the brand's performance and consumer feedback post-launch is crucial for making necessary adjustments. Analyzing metrics, gauging consumer sentiment, and gathering insights enable brands to adapt strategies, address challenges, and capitalize on opportunities. Continuous improvement ensures that the brand remains relevant and resonates with the evolving needs of the audience.

9) **Scaling and Expansion Strategies:**
Once the brand gains traction, scaling and expansion strategies come into play. These strategies involve leveraging the initial success, expanding into new markets or product lines, and capitalizing on brand equity. Brands like Tesla expanded their

product line from electric cars to energy solutions, utilizing their brand equity and success in the automotive market.

10) Long-Term Brand Building and Evolution:

Beyond the initial launch, the focus shifts to long-term brand building and evolution. This involves sustaining brand momentum, fostering innovation, and evolving strategies to stay competitive. Long-term success relies on consistent brand reinforcement, innovation, and adaptability to changing market dynamics.

2.7 Rebranding:

Rebranding is a strategic process undertaken by a company to redefine its brand identity, values, and positioning in the market. It involves making significant changes to various elements such as the brand name, logo, visual identity, messaging, and even the overall brand strategy. The primary objective of rebranding is to revitalise and rejuvenate the brand to better align with the evolving market trends, consumer preferences, or the company's evolving goals.

2.7.1 Meaning:

Rebranding is a strategic overhaul of a company's brand identity, encompassing a comprehensive transformation of its visual elements, messaging, and positioning in the market. It's a deliberate effort to redefine how a brand is perceived by its audience, often driven by shifts in market dynamics, consumer preferences, or the need for a refreshed image. It involves revamping key brand elements like logos, color schemes, and messaging to realign with evolving goals, target demographics, or to differentiate from competitors.

2.7.2 Definitions:

Following are the definitions of the Rebranding:

1) **Al Ries and Laura Ries:**

   "Rebranding is changing the promise a brand makes to its customers. A brand is more than a name, logo, or slogan. It's the set of expectations that customers associate with a product or service."

2) **Philip Kotler:**

   "Rebranding is a marketing strategy in which a new name, term, symbol, design, or combination thereof is created for an established brand with the intention of developing a new, differentiated identity in the minds of consumers."

3) **David A. Aaker:**

   "Rebranding is the process by which a product or service developed with one brand or company or product line affiliation is marketed or distributed with a different identity."

2.7.3 Process of Rebranding:

Equity Rebranding is a strategic process that involves reshaping the identity, perception, and positioning of a brand in the market. It's a multi-faceted undertaking that requires careful planning, execution, and communication.

1) **Assessment and Research:**

   Before diving into a rebrand, it's crucial to assess the current brand position, market trends, audience perceptions, and competitor landscape. Conducting thorough market research, surveys, and interviews can provide valuable insights into what's working and what needs improvement. Understanding your target audience's preferences, pain points, and expectations is pivotal. Analyzing industry trends and competitor strategies can highlight gaps or opportunities that your rebrand can leverage.

2) **Define Objectives and Strategy:**

   Clearly outline the goals and objectives of the rebranding effort. Whether it's to expand market reach, modernize the brand image, or reposition the brand in a changing market, having specific, measurable, achievable, relevant, and time-bound (SMART) goals is essential. Craft a comprehensive strategy that aligns with these objectives. Determine the rebranding scope, including visual identity, messaging, brand voice, and any operational changes required.

3) **Develop Brand Identity:**

   A crucial aspect of rebranding is refining or creating a new brand identity. This includes the logo, color palette, typography, and design elements. It should reflect the brand's values, mission, and resonate with the target audience. Collaborate with designers and brand strategists to create a cohesive visual identity that communicates the essence of the brand effectively.

4) **Refine Messaging and Positioning:**

   Reevaluate the brand's messaging to ensure it aligns with the new identity and resonates with the intended audience. Develop a compelling brand story that communicates the brand's values, uniqueness, and relevance to consumers. Crafting a strong positioning statement that differentiates the brand from competitors is crucial. This statement should clearly articulate what sets the brand apart and why consumers should choose it.

5) **Internal Alignment and Training:**

   Engage and align internal stakeholders, including employees, with the rebranding initiative. Communicate the reasons behind the rebrand, its goals, and the expected impact on the organization. Training sessions may be necessary to ensure everyone embodies the new brand identity in their interactions, reinforcing consistency across all touchpoints.

6) **Execution and Implementation:**

Implement the new brand elements across all touchpoints consistently. This includes updating marketing materials, website, social media profiles, packaging, signage, and any other customer-facing assets. Ensure a phased rollout plan to manage the transition smoothly, minimizing confusion among customers and stakeholders.

7) **Communication and Marketing:**

Develop a comprehensive communication strategy to unveil the rebrand to the market. This may include press releases, social media campaigns, events, and advertisements. Clearly communicate the reasons for the rebrand and how it will benefit consumers. Engage with the audience, seek feedback, and address any concerns transparently.

8) **Gather Feedback and Iterate:**

Monitor and collect feedback from customers, employees, and other stakeholders after the rebranding launch. Analyze this feedback to understand how the new brand is perceived and if any adjustments are needed. Continuous iteration based on feedback ensures the brand stays relevant and resonates with its audience.

9) **Measure Success:**

Define key performance indicators (KPIs) to measure the success of the rebranding effort. Metrics like increased brand awareness, customer engagement, sales growth, and market share can indicate the effectiveness of the rebrand. Regularly track these metrics to gauge the impact of the rebrand and make informed decisions for future strategies.

10) **Long-term Maintenance and Evolution:**

A rebranding effort doesn’t end with the launch. It requires ongoing maintenance and evolution to stay relevant in a dynamic market. Regularly revisit the brand strategy, adapt to market changes, and innovate to maintain brand freshness and relevance.

2.8 Types of Branding:

Each type of branding serves different purposes and requires unique strategies to create a distinctive brand identity, resonate with the target audience, and achieve specific business objectives.

1) **Product Branding:**

Product branding focuses on individual products within a company's portfolio. It involves creating a unique identity, personality, and perception for each product to differentiate it from competitors and resonate with its target audience. Product branding encompasses elements like packaging design, product naming, and specific marketing strategies tailored to highlight the product's features and benefits. Successful product branding often leads to strong customer loyalty and recognition for that specific product in the market.

2) Corporate Branding:

Corporate branding revolves around the overall image, values, and reputation of the entire company. It aims to establish a cohesive identity that reflects the organization's mission, values, and culture. Corporate branding involves creating a consistent visual identity, messaging, and brand positioning across all company touchpoints. It's crucial for building trust, credibility, and long-term relationships with stakeholders, including customers, employees, investors, and the community.

3) Service Branding:

Service branding pertains to businesses that offer intangible services rather than tangible products. It focuses on creating a distinct identity for the services offered, emphasizing the unique value proposition, quality, and customer experience. Service branding often relies on testimonials, word-of-mouth, and customer satisfaction to build trust and credibility. Establishing a strong service brand can differentiate a company in a competitive market and drive customer loyalty.

4) Personal Branding:

Personal branding is about individuals cultivating their own brand identity. It involves creating a unique persona, expertise, and reputation in a particular field or industry. Personal branding utilizes social media, networking, content creation, and public appearances to establish credibility, trust, and recognition. Professionals, influencers, and thought leaders often leverage personal branding to enhance career opportunities, attract opportunities, and build a loyal following.

5) Digital Branding:

With the increasing dominance of the digital landscape, digital branding focuses on establishing and managing a brand's presence online. It encompasses elements such as website design, social media branding, online advertising, content creation, and search engine optimization (SEO). Digital branding aims to create a consistent and engaging brand experience across various digital channels, enabling companies to connect with their audience effectively in the digital realm.

6) Cultural Branding:

Cultural branding aligns the brand with societal or cultural movements, values, or trends. Brands that engage in cultural branding often associate themselves with causes, social issues, or cultural phenomena that resonate with their target audience. By tapping into cultural relevance, brands can create emotional connections with consumers and demonstrate their commitment to causes beyond profit, fostering brand loyalty among socially conscious consumers.

7) Retail Branding:

Retail branding focuses on creating a unique and memorable shopping experience for customers. It involves designing store layouts, ambiance, customer service standards, and exclusive offers to create a distinct brand experience. Successful retail branding not only attracts customers but also encourages repeat visits and builds brand loyalty by providing a consistent and enjoyable shopping environment.

8) **Employer Branding:**

Employer branding is centered on creating a positive image and reputation as an employer. It involves showcasing the company's culture, values, opportunities for career growth, and employee benefits to attract and retain top talent. Strong employer branding can differentiate a company in a competitive job market, leading to higher employee satisfaction, lower turnover rates, and a stronger workforce.

2.9 Branding in Graphic Design:

Branding in graphic design plays a pivotal role in shaping a brand's visual identity and perception in the eyes of consumers.

1) **Logo Design:**

The logo is the cornerstone of a brand's visual identity. Graphic designers play a crucial role in creating logos that encapsulate the essence of a brand – its values, personality, and offerings. Logos are designed to be memorable, versatile, and instantly recognizable, serving as a visual anchor for the brand. Through careful consideration of colors, typography, symbols, and layout, designers craft logos that resonate with the target audience and convey the brand's identity effectively.

2) **Visual Identity Systems:**

Graphic designers establish comprehensive visual identity systems that govern how a brand appears across various platforms and mediums. This includes defining color palettes, typography guidelines, iconography, imagery styles, and layout principles. Consistency is key in these guidelines to ensure cohesive and recognizable brand communication. Designers create style guides that serve as reference documents for internal and external stakeholders, ensuring that every visual element aligns with the brand's identity.

3) **Branding Collateral:**

Graphic design extends to creating various branding collateral, such as business cards, letterheads, brochures, and packaging. These materials are essential touchpoints that reinforce the brand's identity and leave a lasting impression on customers. Designers employ their skills to harmonize the brand's visual elements across these collaterals, maintaining consistency and professionalism while effectively communicating the brand's message and values.

4) **Digital Branding:**

In today's digital age, graphic design plays a critical role in shaping a brand's online presence. Designers create compelling visuals for websites, social media platforms, email campaigns, and digital advertisements. They ensure that the brand's visual identity remains consistent across these digital channels, optimizing graphics for different screen sizes and platforms. Engaging and visually appealing digital designs enhance user experience, reinforce brand recognition, and drive online engagement.

5) **Packaging Design:**
Packaging is a tangible representation of a brand that directly interacts with consumers. Graphic designers create packaging designs that not only protect the product but also communicate the brand's story, values, and unique selling propositions. Design elements like colors, typography, imagery, and structural design work together to attract attention on the shelf, convey information, and evoke emotions, influencing purchasing decisions.

6) **Brand Communication Materials:**
From advertisements to promotional materials, graphic design is instrumental in crafting effective brand communication. Whether it's designing print ads, banners, or digital marketing visuals, designers ensure that every piece of communication aligns with the brand's identity and messaging. Through compelling visuals and cohesive design language, these materials convey the brand's story and offerings, ultimately connecting with the audience on an emotional level.

7) **User Interface (UI) and User Experience (UX) Design:**
UI/UX design is integral to digital products and services. Graphic designers contribute to creating intuitive, visually appealing interfaces that enhance the user experience. By focusing on layout, visual hierarchy, color schemes, and interactive elements, designers ensure that the brand's digital touchpoints offer a seamless and engaging experience that reflects the brand's identity and values.

8) **Brand Evolution and Adaptation:**
As brands evolve or expand, graphic designers play a crucial role in adapting the visual identity to reflect these changes while maintaining brand consistency. Whether it's a brand refresh, expansion into new markets, or catering to evolving consumer preferences, designers reinterpret and evolve the brand's visual elements to stay relevant while preserving its core identity.

2.10 Branding in the Age of Social Media:

Branding in the age of social media is a multifaceted endeavor that leverages the power of digital platforms to shape brand perception, engage audiences, and drive business objectives.

1) **Brand Presence Across Platforms:**
Social media provides a myriad of platforms like Facebook, Instagram, Twitter, LinkedIn, TikTok, and others, allowing brands to establish a presence where their audience engages the most. Each platform offers unique demographics and content formats, influencing how brands communicate. Brands strategically choose platforms aligned with their target demographics, adapting content to suit each platform's nuances while maintaining a consistent brand voice and identity.

2) **Content Creation and Strategy:**
Social media revolves around content. Brands create tailored content strategies that resonate with their audience, considering the platform's algorithms and user behaviors. Visual content, videos, infographics, user-generated content, and interactive elements are designed by social media teams or designers to capture attention, drive engagement, and convey the brand's message effectively.

3) **Community Engagement and Interaction:**
Social media enables direct interaction between brands and their audience, fostering a sense of community. Brands actively engage with their followers through comments, direct messages, polls, and live sessions. This engagement builds brand loyalty, trust, and brand advocates as users feel heard and valued, contributing to a positive brand image.

4) **Influencer Partnerships and Collaborations:**
Brands leverage influencers and content creators to amplify their reach and credibility. Collaborating with influencers aligning with the brand's values and target audience enables access to a larger and more engaged audience. Graphic designers often contribute by creating branded content that fits seamlessly into influencers' feeds, maintaining brand consistency while leveraging the influencer's unique style.

5) **Real-time Marketing and Trends:**
Social media thrives on trends and real-time conversations. Brands monitor trending topics and participate in conversations relevant to their industry or audience interests. Designers play a role in quickly creating visually engaging content that aligns with these trends, ensuring brands stay relevant and responsive in the fast-paced social media landscape.

6) **Brand Advocacy and User-Generated Content (UGC):**
Brands encourage user-generated content by showcasing customer experiences, reviews, and testimonials. Designers often create templates or branded frames encouraging users to share content related to the brand. UGC serves as authentic endorsements, strengthening brand credibility and fostering a community where customers become advocates.

7) **Paid Advertising and Visual Storytelling:**
Social media advertising allows precise targeting based on demographics, interests, and behaviors. Designers craft visually compelling ads that stand out amidst the noise, conveying the brand's message succinctly and persuasively. Visual storytelling through ads or sponsored content helps evoke emotions, driving engagement and conversions.

8) **Data Analytics and Insights:**
Social media platforms offer robust analytics tools that provide valuable insights into audience behavior, content performance, and campaign effectiveness. Brands

leverage these insights to refine their strategies and optimize content. Designers collaborate with analytics teams to understand which visuals resonate best with the audience, informing future design choices.

9) **Crisis Management and Reputation Building:**
Social media can magnify both positive and negative brand experiences. Brands need to respond promptly to customer feedback, reviews, or crises. Designers may assist in creating visually appealing, empathetic, and informative responses or statements during challenging times, contributing to effective crisis management and reputation building.

10) **Consistency and Adaptability:**
Maintaining a consistent brand presence while adapting to the dynamic social media landscape is crucial. Designers ensure that visuals, branding elements, and messaging remain consistent across various social media channels while also staying flexible to adapt to evolving trends, platform changes, and audience preferences.

❖❖❖❖❖

Multiple Choice Questions

1) **------------ is the process of creating and enhancing the perception of a brand in the minds of consumers.**
a) Innovation b) Branding c) Hoarding d) Neglect
2) **------------ involve planned actions to strengthen a brand's position and image in the market.**
a) Collaboration b) Strategies c) Ignorance d) Arbitration
3) **The impact of advertising in building brand equity is significant in shaping consumer ------------.**
a) Communication b) Experiences c) Hoarding d) Ignorance
4) **Effective marketing communications contribute to ------------ and enhancing a brand's identity.**
a) Collaboration b) Hoarding c) Positioning d) Exploitation
5) **Growing and sustaining brands require consistent efforts in maintaining brand ------------ and relevance.**
a) Innovation b) Elements c) Hoarding d) Equity
6) **Process internal branding focuses on aligning employees with the ------------ and values of a brand.**
a) Collaboration b) Hoarding c) Ignorance d) Strategy

7) Successful new brand launches involve creating a ------------ that resonates with the target audience.

a) Hoarding b) Communication

c) Positioning d) Strategy

8) ------------ is the process of giving a brand a new identity or image to revitalize its market presence.

a) Rebranding b) Innovation c) Hoarding d) Ignorance

9) Types of branding include personal branding, corporate branding, and ----------- - branding.

a) Collaboration b) Hoarding c) Product d) Exploitation

10) Branding in graphic design involves creating visual elements that represent a brand's ------------.

a) Innovation b) Identity c) Hoarding d) Neglect

11) Branding in the age of social media requires active ------------ and engagement with online communities.

a) Communication b) Collaboration c) Ignorance d) Hoarding

12) Brand building is crucial for creating a unique ------------ for a product or service.

a) Innovation b) Hoarding c) Identity d) Arbitration

13) Brand building strategies aim to create a strong ------------ and emotional connection with consumers.

a) Collaboration b) Hoarding c) Positioning d) Ignorance

14) The impact of advertising in building brand equity extends to creating brand ------------ and loyalty.

a) Experiences b) Communication

c) Hoarding d) Innovation

15) Marketing communications play a key role in conveying the ------------ and values of a brand.

a) Collaboration b) Identity c) Ignorance d) Hoarding

16) Growing and sustaining brands involve adapting to ------------ market trends and consumer preferences.

a) Innovation b) Hoarding

c) Communication d) Arbitration

17) Process internal branding ensures that employees embody the ------------ of the brand in their actions.

a) Collaboration b) Hoarding c) Ignorance d) Strategy

18) Successful new brand launches require a clear understanding of the target audience and effective ------------.

a) Hoarding b) Communication c) Positioning d) Strategy

19) Rebranding is a strategic decision aimed at ------------ a brand's image and market perception.

a) Innovation b) Hoarding c) Ignorance d) Arbitration

20) Types of branding include personal branding, corporate branding, and ------------ branding.

a) Collaboration b) Hoarding c) Product d) Exploitation

21) Branding in graphic design involves creating visual elements that represent a brand's ------------.

a) Innovation b) Identity c) Hoarding d) Neglect

22) Branding in the age of social media requires active ------------ and engagement with online communities.

a) Communication b) Collaboration c) Ignorance d) Hoarding

23) Brand building is crucial for creating a unique ------------ for a product or service.

a) Innovation b) Hoarding c) Identity d) Arbitration

24) Brand building strategies aim to create a strong ------------ and emotional connection with consumers.

a) Collaboration b) Hoarding c) Positioning d) Ignorance

25) The impact of advertising in building brand equity extends to creating brand ------------ and loyalty.

a) Experiences b) Communication c) Hoarding d) Innovation

26) Marketing communications play a key role in conveying the ------------ and values of a brand.

a) Collaboration b) Identity c) Ignorance d) Hoarding

27) Growing and sustaining brands involve adapting to ------------ market trends and consumer preferences.

a) Innovation b) Hoarding

c) Communication d) Arbitration

28) Process internal branding ensures that employees embody the ------------ of the brand in their actions.

a) Collaboration b) Hoarding c) Ignorance d) Strategy

29) Successful new brand launches require a clear understanding of the target audience and effective ------------.

a) Hoarding b) Communication

c) Positioning d) Strategy

30) Rebranding is a strategic decision aimed at ------------ a brand's image and market perception.

a) Innovation **b)** Hoarding **c)** Ignorance **d)** Arbitration

Ans : **1)** b, **2)** b, **3)** b, **4)** a, **5)** c, **6)** a, **7)** d, **8)** a, **9)** c, **10)** b, **11)** b, **12)** c, **13)** a, **14)** a, **15)** b, **16)** a, **17)** a, **18)** b, **19)** a, **20)** c, **21)** b, **22)** b, **23)** c, **24)** a, **25)** a, **26)** b, **27)** a, **28)** a, **29)** b, **30)** a.

❖❖❖❖❖

Review Questions

Q. 1. What is mean by Brand Building? State the Importance of Brand Building.

Q. 2. Explain the Brand Building Strategies in detail.

Q. 3. Discuss about Impact of Advertising in Building Brand Equity.

Q. 4. Explain in detail about Marketing Communications and Brand Building.

Q. 5. Write in detail about the Growing Brands.

Q. 6. Discuss in detail about the Sustaining Brands.

Q. 7. Explain in detail about Process Internal Branding.

Q. 8. Write in detail about New Brand Launches.

Q. 9. What is mean by Rebranding? Explain Process of Rebranding.

Q. 10 State the types of Branding.

Q. 11 Discuss in detail about Branding in Graphic Design.

Q. 12 Write about Branding in the Age of the Social Media.

Q. 13. Write Short Notes on Following:

a) Brand Building.

b) Growing Brands.

c) Sustaining Brands.

d) Process Internal Branding.

e) Rebranding.

f) Branding in Graphic Design.

❖❖❖❖❖